California's
APPLE
BLOSSOM
TRAIL

WHEN THE APPLE WAS KING
AND CHILDREN RESILIENT

DANIEL DAWSON

California's Apple Blossom Trail:
When the Apple was King and Children Resilient
© 2022, Daniel Dawson. All rights reserved.
Published by Apple Blossom Press, Sebastopol, CA

ISBN 979-8-9856092-0-2 (paperback)
ISBN 979-8-9856092-1-9 (eBook)
Library of Congress Control Number: 2022901533

Publication managed by AuthorImprints.com

Dedicated to my four Daughters,
Elizabeth, Melissa, Melody, and Amy

Contents

Down on the Corner

I FELT LIKE THE LUCKIEST kid alive to have the wide-open spaces of our apple orchard West of the small town of Sebastopol in Northern California and the playgrounds at Twin Hills School on which to play. I had places where I could be alone and safe, surrounded only by trees and the big blue sky! The corner of the orchard within our 1910 house was the center of my life compass. Out the backdoor to the dusty driveway, I could go left and walk up past the tall, white water tower, topped with a wind compass that added to its already tall stature. The tallest building around, it was home to a family of white barn owls up the fifteen wooden steps on the inside ladder.

A few yards away stood a huge, old weathered red barn. The western face of the barn served as the outfield fence when my brothers and I played baseball on our long gravelly driveway. A long hit of the ball, from down by the house, that reached the barn wall with a resounding pop, was dubbed an automatic home run!

Up in the big red barn, among dusty relics of over fifty years of apple farming, hunted for old nails, bolts, rope, and wood to use in making "apple box racers," along with anything else that looked interesting and curious. Up on the top deck of the barn, in what was the hayloft when horse-drawn wagons brought apples here from the surrounding orchard, we found a very interesting, if not potentially fatal, relic of the bygone farming era.

Before tractors and backhoes were invented, the preferred method to remove old, unwanted tree stumps was dynamite. How long this dusty, wooden box had been up there we didn't know, but the three of us—myself, a curious 11 year old, and my brothers Richie, 10, and John, 9—recognized the potential immediately. After all, we were faithful Saturday morning cartoon viewers and had seen Wile E. Coyote use dynamite many times in his quest to put an end to his nemesis, the Road Runner. Beep! Beep! He just shook off the blasts that resulted when his plots against the Road Runner inevitably backfired.

I grabbed a stick of the waxy, grayish paper-wrapped dynamite, curious why it wasn't red like in the movies and cartoons. I took it down the driveway to our backyard and tried to light it with matches I took from Dad's cigarette drawer in the kitchen. The fact that I could have been killed, possibly along with both of my brothers, never crossed my young mind. Nothing happened, even after several attempts. Someone was looking out for us. Not to be discouraged though, we headed back up and got the coil of fuse from the box and played around with that, but it didn't seem to do much either. Eventually, we grew bored and gave up on the whole idea.

Apple box racers, on the other hand, were always an adventure. Our imaginary "Fremont Drag Strip" was a paved, downhill stretch of Watertrough Road, from the barn to the bottom of the hill where Atascadero Creek flowed under the road.

Apple lug boxes were big enough to hold two five-gallon buckets and measured about twenty-four inches long by fourteen inches wide and eight inches deep. We nailed a three-foot long two by four on the bottom, in the back, and used old lawnmower or bicycle wheels nailed into the ends of the two by four as a rear axle. The front axle was a little more complicated since steering was very important. A two by four about the same length as the one used for the rear axle was mounted to the bottom and front of the lug box by drilling a hole through the center of the board and one through the box bottom using a hand drill, the kind with a wooden handle in the middle and a wood knob on top that you turn like a butter churn. We attached it with a bolt, washers, and a nut scrounged from inside the barn or the pumphouse. Out near the front wheel of each side a knotted rope was tied, and a nail bent to hold it in place, which allowed the driver to steer by pulling the rope left or right.

We had John drive first, since he was the smallest and lightest of the three of us. If the wheels didn't collapse with John in the cockpit, then we normally progressed by weight and age, so next came Richie and finally me. The weak link in our boyhood engineering design was the way the wheels were nailed into the wooden axles. Attached with only several small nails, they were prone to collapse at any time, usually both at once with the wheels assuming a pigeon-toed failure. Sometimes they would hold up for several yards down the driveway, Richie and me pushing John along and yelling at him to keep the rope "reins" steering system straight.

Our apple box coaster design was gradually improved upon after noting the weak points and scrounging up stronger materials for another try. No foresight was given to the fact that brakes might be needed after a successful run down Watertrough.

For the newest iteration of the apple box racer, I found a couple of nice twelve-inch nails that would make perfect axles, along with various nuts, bolts, and washers. This time, I was determined the wheels would hold the weight given the strength of the twelve-inch nails! Excitedly, I assembled the front axle using the newfound parts and attached it to the apple box, doubling over two nails to secure the steering rope to the two by four front axle.

"OK, Bones (John's nickname), get in and let's see if this thing's gonna work," I said. John hopped into the cockpit with a smile; he got to ride while Richie and I pushed. The test run—about thirty yards of dirt driveway from the garage up to the barn—was a success and the wheels looked sturdy. So far, so good.

We were ready for phase two of the road test, but I was tired of seeing the wheels collapse when I got in the box, so I insisted that my smaller and lighter brother, Bones stay in and first test drive it down Watertrough Road. I grabbed the steering rope and towed the racer up the driveway to the barn and over to the paved road. Richie and I got behind the apple box racer, while Bones took his place behind the wheel. I handed him the steering rope. "Just keep it straight and if any cars come, stay over to the right, OK?" I instructed him. Bones, eager to roll, said, "OK, got it, now let's go!"

The start was easy given the gradual downhill slope, but we underestimated how quickly the racer would pick up speed once it reached the downhill pavement, having only used the dirt driveway thus far in our racer development careers. Bones was all smiles as the hot new racer cruised along, wind in his face and happy to be first at something for once in his life.

I imagined that his smile soon turned to a serious expression as the speed increased, and the steering became sensitive. "Keep it straight!" I yelled from the top of the hill. Suddenly, Bone's seriousness turned to full-fledged panic as the racer was smoking down that hill and Bones, probably for the first time, realized that he had no way to stop it. Richie and I were whooping it up now, yelling words of encouragement as we also came to the same realization: no brakes!

All our efforts to get the racer to go, and yet we didn't think that maybe we would want it to stop! Just as I repeated, "Keep it straight," Bones went into full panic mode as the racer went into a high-speed wobble as he wildly jerked the steering rope with his small, sweaty hands. He panicked and jerked the right steering rope when he spotted an oncoming car, which sent him and the racer flying off the road and into a ditch covered with blackberry bushes.

The berry vines that quickly wrapped around Bones and the tangled racer provided ample stopping power, but the two were soon separated. When the racer stopped, Bones flew about twenty more feet into a thicket of berries. Richie and I laughed and whooped as we ran down the hill to see if our brother was hurt and, more importantly, to survey the damage to the apple box racer!

Bones was crying and laughing at the same time. He was covered with bloody scratches from the berry vines and a few ripe berries had left their purple marks across his forearms and neck as well. "I told you to keep it straight, what happened?" I asked as I pulled him out of the ditch. "It wwaa-was going t-too fast and a cc-car was coming!" he blurted out, between cries. Richie and I were out of breath and excited by the semi-successful test run. Our excitement and laughter soothed "pilot Bones" as we congratulated him.

A lady in a Ford station wagon that had caused John to panic and jerk the racer into the ditch had stopped and asked if we were OK. She had a concerned look when she saw Bones bleeding and crying. "He's all right ma'am, just ran into some berries, that's all. We live just up the hill, so we'll get him home and cleaned up," I said.

She drove away slowly, looking doubtful and concerned, as Bones continued to pout softly and pick at his bloody scratches. We untangled him and the racer and looked back up the hill toward home. "Come on, Bones, don't be a pussy. Richie, pull it back up the hill, next time I'll drive it!" Back up the hill we went, semi-successful apple box engineers.

By the barn there was a small, seasonal labor camp, built many years ago for the Mexican workers who showed up during harvest time.

The labor camp was a circle of four, small one-room cabins with a few metal box spring bed frames covered by thin mattresses and a single lightbulb hanging from the ceiling. They each had four convertible, glassless "windows" made of solid wood panels that could be opened on hot days to let in the cool air. There was a very small communal kitchen a few yards from the cabins that contained a stove, sink, refrigerator, and some cupboard space for dry food storage.

The apple dryer towered a short one hundred feet from the labor camp. Apple dryers once dotted the surrounding landscape and were used to dehydrate apples prior to the advent of canning and refrigeration. Our dryer stood at the top of the hill on Watertrough Road, and its cement and rusted metal smokestack could be seen for miles around. The building was eventually repurposed as the new labor camp with one dorm-style sleeping room and a large kitchen/dining room. There were showers downstairs and outside the building which the old camp lacked. This grand old structure, built like a wooden naval warship with thick slabs of knotless redwood planks, was built to last. The wooden drying racks, measuring twenty-feet across and thirty-feet deep, were still intact in the cement underbelly of the building, and it was easy to imagine them full of apple rounds cut to dry. The boys in WWII must have loved the taste of good old American apples out on the battlefields of Europe because apparently, according to historical accounts, tons of them were dried and shipped out during the war years.

Across from the dryer was the small house where ranch foreman, Don Domingo, lived. Surrounded in the middle of the orchard by tall piles of pruned apple branches, he would wave and smile when we walked or bicycled past the house on our way to the canyon. My brothers and I always felt sad that he was there all alone, leaving for Mexico in the winter and returning in the spring to prepare for another season. One spring, he returned with his whole family to stay, his wife and eight kids—Hector, Antonio, Sophia, Maribelle, Mooko, the twins Jose and Domingo, and Maria—all shared that modest, two bedroom house. Mama Domingo made a nice stack of handmade corn tortillas every day and once we befriended the kids, we were allowed to stop by and buy a rolled-up tortilla with sugar for a penny.

Mooko and the twins were energetic and a few years younger than my brothers. They loved to play a game of coin flip with their tortilla proceeds. Pennies were flipped into the air by each boy in the three-person game, and the one who flipped odd would win the other two pennies; if all three flipped and landed on heads, then everyone reflipped; if all three pennies came up tails we reflipped, and eventually there would be an odd heads among two tails, or a tails among two heads and a winner collected the others pennies. Sometimes nickels and "dimees" were used depending on how rich and how lucky we were each feeling that day, and on very rare occasions we'd use a quarter.

The best part of having those kids as neighbors was that I learned Spanish and they added to their English vocabulary in return. The dirty words were the first to be translated: puto (manwhore, coward, or traitor) was tossed around a lot. We were told La Migra (immigration) would send all the field hands running for the hills and that we shouldn't use it jokingly. Panocha (pussy or vagina) and verga (dick or cock) were staples as were the old favorites, chinga tu madre! (fuck your mother!), pinche cabron (fucking asshole), and hijo de la chingada (son of a bitch). We laughed and translated all the dirty words we knew and then moved on to more useful, everyday definitions like tree (arbol), brothers (hermanos), school (escuela), and food (comida). I loved learning Spanish and practiced speaking and reading the language during the coming years. It was an easy A all through high school, and I even skipped two years because it was so easy. I used the language even more when I started working at the local flea market when I was fifteen years old, selling fresh produce that I'd also helped pick in the orchards and fields of the Central and Imperial Valleys of California.

The canyon in the middle of the orchard, surrounded by the pruned branches, was basically the end of a large drainage pipe that surfaced after traveling underground for several acres from the top corner of the orchard. The old, rusty steel pipe had rivets connecting the seams. We called it the submarine because that's what it looked like to a group of small boys with vivid imaginations. The erosion over the years had created our own small-scale version of the Grand Canyon, made deeper by the ten-foot-high stacks of prunings that surrounded its perimeter. The canyon was a great hiding place and playground for all of us kids. We split up into teams and hunted each other by throwing apples. Funny how we could spend all day just playing around, making up imaginative games, and creating something from nothing outside in the sunshine.

The bottom of the orchard was bordered by Atascadero Creek, a natural discovery playground in and of itself. Turtles, frogs, water skeeters, birds, dragonflies, and raccoons all clamored for survival in the life-giving waters. Willow trees and blackberry bushes lined the banks, along with an occasional troublesome patch of the dreaded poison oak bush. There were pools and rapids but few were deep enough for swimming. We drank the cool water and picked the sweet, dark, ripe blackberries in the heat of summer. Jammed up broken limbs created what looked like bank to bank thick beaver dams full of debris from upstream. These held back the raging winter waters and created deep pools that allowed fast moving waters to trickle through like waterfalls.

The tall willow trees created a cave-like effect at the water level, allowing only a limited amount of filtered sunlight to reach the creek itself. The cool and sandy mini-beaches were a perfect place to sit in the shade during a hot summer day and daydream as the sound of trickling water filled the air. A safe place, peaceful, cool, and quiet. Even my sister Debbie's horses knew this was a safe place, because every time the horses became restless during a storm, they broke out of the corral or barn and headed down there, under the cover of trees along the creek.

The creek itself was a natural paradise but the real gold mine was upstream, along the creek bank bordering the bottom of Furusho's orchard. There were long, tall heaps of garbage and a tremendous variety of discarded items lining the bank for what seemed like a mile. Furusho's dump was where my curiosity and sense of wonder came alive, a veritable treasure hunt on every visit!

Household garbage of rotting food, tin cans, shitty diapers, broken toys, appliances, car parts, tires, and all varieties of trash were brought here from who knows where. The treasures for my brothers and me were the returnable Coke bottles worth five cents each. We competed for them as if they were golden eggs in an Easter egg hunt. Lots of the bottles were marked "No Deposit—No Return" and since they had no value, they were thrown into the slow moving waters of the creek and used as target practice. We'd throw a bottle at them in an attempt to hit one and shatter the glass.

Steve Furusho, my classmate Mark's older brother, was a high schooler interested in fast cars, as evidenced by the many boxes of *Hot Rod* and *Super Dragster* magazines that I retrieved from the garbage pile and took back up the hill to our house. These were flame-throwing long dragsters with long bodies and gigantic fat tires in the back and small skinny ones up front that the driver couldn't see because of the huge engine in front of him. Funny cars and their drivers with names like Big Daddy and the Mongoose, Don Prudhomme, the Snake driving his Hot Wheels Barracuda, Jungle Jim, and the Hawaiian filled the pages with action shots on the dragstrips of California. Boxes of discarded baseball cards were reclaimed with enthusiasm too! All the greats of the 1960s including my favorite team, the San Francisco Giants—Willie Mays, Willie McCovey, Juan Marichal, Chris Speier—all tossed into the trash. Mana from heaven for me! I hoofed it up the hill and stowed my treasures in the bedroom closet, to be inspected and savored later when the time was right. These journeys of discovery became an almost every weekend occurrence for my brothers and me, as nobody wanted to miss out on a new returnable Coke bottle or other treasure. I latched on to anything with wheels. Broken bicycles, baby carriages, carts, toys, dollies, lawn mowers, or anything that might help me fabricate one of our apple box racers. As the old saying goes, one man's trash is another man's treasure!

The apple ranch and the open countryside were nature's bounty and my salvation and means of survival physically, mentally, and spiritually. Everything was within walking distance and the center of the universe as far as I was concerned. I could depend on things being in place and consistent—the land, trees, creek, and the Twin Hills School playgrounds—all unchanging and here to stay. Somehow, we were protected from harm by an unknown and unseen benevolent source, through the innocence of youth, exploring and growing up and being kids on the ranch.

The Cupcake Crew

THE COOL, FRESH MORNING FOG dampened the sound of apples hitting the bottoms of the five-gallon plastic buckets, unseen, somewhere up in the orchard. The sound was like a series of tribal drumbeats performed by out of sync drummers. The faster the beat, the more windfallen apples were going from the soft powdery soil, through eager adolescent hands, and into the buckets.

The buckets were quickly emptied into a wooden bin that held about fifty of those five-gallon buckets, or the equivalent of a thousand pounds of Gravenstein apples.

An early-season variety, Gravenstein apples are ready to harvest in mid-July. They offer the perfect opportunity for summer jobs for kids willing to do hard work before the start of school in September. The Sonoma County Fair, over in Santa Rosa, coincided with the start of the Gravenstein harvest. The first week's pay was usually spent at the fair on cotton candy, corn dogs, carnival rides, and games.

It was a common six-week summer job out in the apple orchards of Sebastopol, and kids like my brothers and me could earn enough money to buy some school clothes. At nine cents a bucket, a kid could make one hundred dollars or so for the season and that went a long way in 1974. In fact, the monthly rent for our farmhouse on the sixty-acre apple ranch was one hundred dollars.

The "Boss Lady," a.k.a. Jean Megini, came up with a clever name for our crew the previous summer. During one of her trips to the orchard where we were picking and down to the big red barn on her yellow Massey Ferguson tractor, she exchanged two full apple bins for two empty ones. Upon her return, she spotted our crew taking a short break, talking, as we all sat on our overturned buckets in a circle.

As the tractor approached the waiting crew, Boss Lady laughingly announced, "You jaybirds look like half a dozen cupcakes, the way you were all sitting on your buckets in a circle! I'm gonna call you jokers the cupcake crew!"

The name stuck. The crew consisted of myself, a fourteen-year-old on top of the world, a teller of these true stories, plus my two little brothers, thirteen-year-old Richie and twelve-year-old John, along with the two Alberdingi brothers.

Robbie Alberdingi was the hardest worker and, at sixteen, the natural leader of the crew. He set the pace, drove the tractor when Jean needed him to, and rounded up the crew when we moved from one orchard to another. He was good natured, funny, and concerned that everyone be treated fairly, a characteristic that came naturally to him as the oldest of his five. His fifteen-year-old brother, Perry, was second in the pecking order and was a bit of a smart ass, most likely because he was always number two, both at home and in the orchard. Perry reminded me frequently that his family, like the Meginis, were proud Italians and that we were second class citizens because we weren't Italian.

The Meginis, George and "Boss Lady" Jean, were our land-lords, as we lived on their Burnside-Watertrough Ranch, and the Alberdingi's lived on their Twin Hills School Ranch, mere steps from our common elementary school. We would often walk up the road to play ball on the playground, with a couple other neighborhood kids, after school and on weekends.

During the heat of the summer of Gravenstein apple season, the crew size occasionally increased with a friend or a relative, brought in temporarily by the Boss Lady. I started picking when I was twelve years old and realized that I had to fit in and gain the approval of the older kids and the Boss Lady to remain employed. She was great with all the kids, mostly because I think she really liked all of us. The Boss Lady was always kind and patient, willing to help one of us fill a bucket to catch up with the older boys or to stick up for someone when an argu-ment broke out to help smooth things over.

The Boss Lady greeted me warmly as I walked up into the upper reaches of the orchard, following the drumbeat sound to find the crew. I came to work late that day, after seeing my grandpa off for his latest round of cancer treatments down at the VA Hospital in Livermore. "Good morning, DJ. Did you get your grandpa on his way?" she asked, as she smiled and looked up at me from her tally book, while sitting on her tractor.

The Boss Lady was the only one who ever called me DJ, and I came to like that nickname. She was privy to my full name, Daniel Joseph, because I went to the post office in Sebastopol to get my social security card, the previous summer of 1973, per her instruction. I was hoping to make at least a hundred dollars that picking season and I learned that Uncle Sam wanted his share. I became a tax paying citizen at age thirteen. That year, the crew switched to lighter, plastic buckets. The previous year, my first, we filled heavy metal buckets.

"Yep, he's headed back to the VA Hospital again," I said solemnly. The Boss Lady looked at me with a smile and said, "He'll be OK, DJ, now get to work before you miss out on all these apples. A good strong wind last night knocked down lots of them, so you better get over there and get your share!" I liked the Boss Lady because I felt she looked out for me and always took my side if I got into a scuffle or argument with the older Perry Alberdingi. She encouraged me to keep my "nose to the grindstone," to save a little of my money if I could, and to care for my family. She knew we had a drunk father who was abusive to his children and wife, and that Mom's job at Longs Drugs in Santa Rosa supported the family. She appreciated my love and care for my grandpa.

I grabbed my bucket from the tractor and headed for the apples that were waiting beneath the trees. I was careful not to get too close to the others, lest I piss them off for "stealing their apples." The crew gave me no greeting whatsoever, not even my two younger brothers. As far as they were concerned, I was only there to compete for apples that could otherwise be counted on their tally.

The Boss Lady wore a wide-brimmed straw hat, off-brand blue jeans, and a men's khaki shirt, along with her brown, low-top work boots. She added a few feminine touches just to remind herself and the cupcake crew that she was a lady. A lady to be respected and listened to with attention and deference, lest we all face the wrath of a tongue lashing from her or, in extreme circumstances, her husband, George!

Gold-framed glasses attached to a shiny gold chain kept them from falling off when she leaned forward to pick up the "grounders." A light coating of pink lipstick and a scarf around her neck completed the womanly touches, but make no mistake about it, she could outwork any of us young boys and we knew it! She had the dexterity to pick up ground apples while bent over at the waist, unlike myself, who picked while down on both knees.

She protected her hands with a pair of white cotton gloves with the palms and fingers covered in small black rubber dots for a sure grip. Most of the crew, including myself, picked barehanded. I liked the natural grip created by the oil and orchard dust that coated the apples. At the end of a workday, you could rub your hands together and peel off the waxy-brown coating as it sluffed off into small, rolled up balls.

The only drawback to picking without gloves was that, on a rare occasion, there would be an unseen honeybee feasting on the juice on the other side of an apple. When you quickly grabbed it to toss into your bucket, there could be a painful bee sting involved.

The Boss Lady frequently chewed Wrigley's Gum and if we were all on good behavior and not fighting, she played a variation of "drawing straws," a game using various lengths of a stick of gum, hidden in her palm. After the apple tally was taken, we gathered around the tractor while Boss Lady held up her hand and we each picked a stick. Whether you drew half, a quarter, or the coveted full stick of gum, was entirely up to chance. The lesson being that sometimes you get lucky and sometimes not, but even the losers got something if they played the game.

I once said, during this game, "I wish I would have picked the middle one," which was revealed when one of my brothers happily discovered it to be the full stick. The Boss Lady replied, "If wishes were horses, then beggars would ride, DJ!" A saying I took to heart and translated as, "Be thankful for what you've got, and it's a combination of hard work and good luck that makes things happen!"

During these occasional breaks when Jean took the tally, we traded stories or jokes while passing around a jug of ice water. The Boss Lady put plastic gallon milk jugs full of water in the freezer the night before, so that by the time the midday sun heated up, there was ice cold water from the melted jugs for the crew to enjoy.

Hot summer days and hard work never hurt anyone, but sometimes the crew grew agitated and overly competitive, which led to bickering, insults, flying apples, and an occasional fist-fight. The Boss Lady maintained her composure and control of the crew if things got out of hand. She could quickly get things under control with her "serious" voice.

Only once did I see her lose her composure and give us a good tongue lashing as her face turned red and she appeared close to tears. I recall clearly that day in the hot summer orchard when the crew pushed her too far. It was a terrible feeling to see her so upset!

I was a natural for throwing apples, a skill that helped hone my accuracy for playing football and baseball. I used those skills to target a newcomer's ass if he needed to be reminded of the pecking order of the crew.

Timing and position were crucial elements to my strategy and the chaos that usually ensued helped break up the monotony of a long, hot day in the orchard.

Any newcomer who picked apples bent over at the waist, with their ass sticking up in the air, was just asking for it! A newcomer who came out here for a casual summer job, who thought this was just a fun time to talk and wander around tossing apples into a bucket, was in for a rude awakening.

The core crew was here to earn money to buy school clothes because our parents had too many mouths to feed and little more beyond the basics. The Alberdingi boys had it better than my brothers and me because their dad actually worked to take care of his family, but they weren't out there for fun either.

You could almost guarantee that when a kid was dropped off by his mom in a shiny new car and timidly approached the waiting crew, he would be sized up and tested.

One such unfortunate was Randy. He was delivered by his mommy in the morning fog wearing a new pair of golf shorts secured by a black leather belt, white tennis shoes, and a dark blue sweater with gold lettered "Cal Bears" on the front. Standing there, looking like he was ready for a rich boys' summer camp, he pushed his thick, black horn-rimmed glasses up on the bridge of his nose.

Randy was toting a shiny, plaid-patterned lunchbox, undoubtedly filled with a balanced meal and lovingly prepared with the finest ingredients. We could hardly hold in our smirks and laughter because we knew he wasn't going to last a day. For the tough and lean cupcake crew, this wasn't a summer diversion or an exercise in the virtues of manual labor to be remembered when you went back to school in the fall; for us, this was serious business. I don't know where the Boss Lady found these kids, but I think she did it as a favor to their parents, and I can't imagine that many of them gave a favorable report after the experience.

The cupcake crew welcomed him, one by one, as the Boss Lady introduced us to a timid, fourteen-year-old Randy. Like a pack of wolves that welcome a sheep, we greeted him warmly and said it was great to have someone new to work with us. Each of us sized him up with a smirk and hints of morbid excitement. Boy, did this kid pick the wrong summer job!

He would have been better off downtown emptying ashtrays at L & L Bowling Lanes or washing dishes at the Pine Cone Café or perhaps sweeping the floor at Carlson's clothing store. Like I said, I almost felt sorry for him. He had city boy written all over his face and had no business being out here on a farm as far as this scrappy crew was concerned.

We played nice with Randy during the morning, watching and waiting for the opportunity to show him his place. Indeed, he was a prime mark for he picked slower than hell, bent over at the knees with that fat ass just begging to be struck by a swiftly flying apple. I waited patiently for Jean to take the full bins away after the next tally, only then would I let one fly.

The tally was taken when both the front and back bins had been filled and were ready for the Boss Lady to drive them down to the waiting truck, next to the water tower by the red barn.

After World War II, when all the other farmers in the area were buying Ford and Chevrolet trucks, George's dad, Andre Megini, went all out and bought the shiny, new light-green Mack Truck. A prominent signature hood ornament—a chrome Mack Bulldog with diamond eyes—proudly led the way.

When our workday was done, Jean tied ropes over the twelve full bins on the truck and drove them north of town, on the Gravenstein Highway, to the Apple Time Cannery. There, at the cannery, local farmers waited patiently in line with the days harvest on their flatbed trucks. After driving over the scale, the bins were unloaded and taken into the cannery to be turned into sauce and juice.

I was honored to be able to ride along at the end of one workday after watching the Boss Lady throw the ropes up over the double-stacked bins and walk around to the other side of the truck to tie the ropes using a "trucker's hitch" that tightened the rope and secured the bins of apples.

The sound of gears churning underneath as the engine moved the loaded Mack slowly down the road and the way Jean shifted gears as we picked up speed was exciting, especially sitting up high on the seat and looking out at the road ahead. The bulldog stood at full alert on the front end of the long hood.

Our thirsty dusty crew passed around a jug full of cold water. Boss Lady sat up on the seat of the tractor, pencil and small notebook in hand, and took the tally.

"Robbie!?" she yelled out. As the senior member of the crew, Robbie Alberdingi replied proudly, "Nineteeen!" Then came his brother Perry and in turn by seniority, me, my brothers, and then finally the newbie Randy. Snide comments often followed the number shouted back to the Boss Lady during the tally. Richie yelled out, "Seventeeeen!" moments after Perry yelled out, "Sixteeeeen!" and then it was game on! "You lying sack of shit!" Perry yelled at Richie. Not one to back down from anyone, despite his small stature, Richie just looked at him and said, "Screw you, Perry, you're just jealous!"

A stern look from the Boss Lady ended the squabbling and on through the tally we went. Despite comments, gestures, or threats back and forth, we all knew that we would be going through this exercise again in short order. If things got out of hand and got physical, the Boss Lady intervened in her authoritative voice and yelled, "Knock it off, you jaybirds. I'm the one paying for the buckets, so worry about yourself!"

She normally wrote down the numbers silently, without comment or reply, knowing that two bins held about a hundred buckets, and when the tally total was 110 buckets, someone was lying! She was very clever, our beloved Boss Lady, and never accused anyone, instead allowing peer pressure to take care of things. On the rare occasion when a situation got out of hand, she would only have to say, "Hey, you jokers, knock it off and get back to work. Everyone call your numbers out loud when you dump your buckets!" We all had great respect for Jean, and when she spoke we listened! We all knew we had to work together and how far we could push it without causing the crew to end up one member short due to bickering. Everyone on the cupcake crew, at one time or another, had said, "I quit!" and walked away. But whoever quit always returned; if they quit in the morning, they'd be back after lunch, and if they quit in the afternoon, they'd be back and ready to go the next morning without a word. The newbies who quit usually never came back.

When Randy's name was called, he mumbled, "I think I had twenty-two." The rest of the crew laughed and looked at him in disgust. It was Randy's first day, and we could all see how slow he was, thinking it would have been surprising if he had ten buckets. To hear him say he had out picked Robbie, who was a hard worker, with twenty-two buckets was just absurd. "Twenty-two in your dreams," said Robbie, adding, "you pick slower than an old lady! I don't think you know how to count, lard ass!" I laughed out loud and added, "There's no way Randy, you're either a cheater or really dumb!" Similar comments followed by the other boys until the Boss Lady told us to mind our own count and be nice to each other. After she intervened to calm things down, she left with the full bins, knowing full well that peer pressure was about to erupt behind her. Away she went on the tractor, carrying the bins down between the rows of apple-filled trees, leaving a trail of powdery dust in the air.

As the crew resumed scouring the ground for more pennies, I took aim at my target—Randy's fat ass—and let 'er rip. Thraaaap! Bullseye!

"Hey! Who threw that?" asked an indignant Randy. The crew all turned toward Randy and then looked at each other, wondering who it was that struck first. I looked at everyone with a big smirk on my face and remained silent. After a moment I refocused my attention on picking apples.

Nobody responded to Randy as they went back to the task at hand. "Well, whoever it was, that's not funny!" Randy announced. Funny is in the eye of the beholder and now the fun had begun! Once that first apple had struck its mark and the crew saw how he responded, it was playtime. Perry waited patiently and then took a shot that let out a dull thud as it found its spot on the back of Randy's leg. Now all of us laughed as Randy stood up, turned around and said, "That's not very nice, that hurt! Who threw that apple at me?" I looked at him and said, "I don't know who threw what, but I guess that's two down and twenty more coming your way, you lying sack of shit!"

Randy was temporarily "saved by the bell" when lunchtime was announced by the noon whistle, up at the Gold Ridge Firehouse. The long low siren sounded throughout the valleys west of Sebastopol, signaling to everyone working outside that it was time for lunch. The Boss Lady arrived and let us know we would be picking up at the Alberdingi's orchard after lunch, next to Twin Hills School.

The crew, followed at a distance by Randy, walked down through the orchard to our house, where Robbie and his brother, Perry, got into Robbie's 1964 Chevy Chevelle Malibu for the short drive up the road to their house. Randy found a shady spot under a tree while my brothers and I went into our house to scrounge up something to eat.

Mom was at work and Dad was over at Leon's Bar in Santa Rosa, as usual, so my brothers and I had a few slices of peanut butter toast for lunch, along with a few swigs of milk out of the carton, before sitting around in the backyard waiting to go back to work. On days when Dad was home, I preferred to eat a couple of apples for lunch and stay away from the house. It was bad enough that he took 20 percent of our earnings for "living under his roof," I didn't need a lunchtime lecture too!

When lunchtime was over the Boss Lady came thumping along on the tractor to retrieve Randy, my brothers, and me. We jumped back into the empty bins for the short ride up the hill to the Alberdingi's house. Randy, apparently ready for more of what the cupcake crew was dishing out, rolled himself into the back bin while my brothers and I rode out front. As the tractor went swiftly up the paved road, the breeze cooled us down, in the heat of the afternoon sun. Riding in the front bin felt like cruising down Main Street in Sebastopol's Apple Blossom Parade that we had all attended back in April.

The Alberdingi boys, Robbie and Perry, met us in front of their house, ready for an eventful afternoon. Randy looked tired and doubtful; he was already sweating, and we hadn't even started picking. We might as well put this poor bastard out of his misery soon. The bullshit tallies he had announced in the morning were just too big an insult to all of us and could not be ignored.

Once under the shady Gravenstein trees, at the upper reaches of the orchard, the crew went to work silently and quickly, devouring the apples from the ground. The drumbeat thump of apples on bucket bottoms intensified. The competition for school money was back in full swing and each of us was determined to outpace the other. All of us, except Randy, that is. He lumbered along without urgency or vigor. Tally time rolled around soon enough, and we each shouted out our numbers as the Boss Lady called out our names. Randy tried once again to cheat, rather than work, for his count.

When he yelled out a number greater than Perry's count, the Boss Lady shook her head and wrote it on her paper tablet. Perry, sweating and scowling, barely stifled a "Bullshit!" as the rest of us stared Randy down and shook our heads in disbelief. Was he really that stupid, or did he think we were stupid?

Once the Boss Lady drove off with the full bins, the diesel engine grew distant and muffled. The crew didn't waste any time addressing Randy's arithmetic problem.

The first apple to strike was a hard green one, thrown with serious intent. Surely that would leave a nice red welt on the back of Randy's thigh. "Ouch, goddammit!" he yelled out in pain as he rolled on the ground.

Perry just looked at him and replied, "That's what cheaters get around here!" Randy stared back and slowly composed himself as he retrieved his spilled bucket and went back to picking. "I'm working just as hard as any of you guys, so just leave me alone!" Randy said angrily. "Working hard, my ass!" I chimed in as I let two rotten apples fly in rapid succession. Each of the semi-soft, juicy beauties found their mark on the back pockets of Randy's white, momma's boy, preppy shorts.

The wet, brown mash splattered like a rotten egg. It looked like Randy had shit his pants. Everyone laughed at the hilarious sight and joined in for a thorough pummeling of the cheater. Rotten apples and green ones alike rained down on the crying and angry Randy, his face red and sweaty. We all watched as he kicked over his bucket and started to walk away. "I quit, you bastards. I don't need this shitty job anyway!" he wailed.

Perry looked at him and said, "Well, take this with you then!" and punched him in the side of the head. Randy just kept moving down the orchard toward the sound of the Boss Lady's tractor. He was gone and did not return the following morning, or ever. Of that we were certain. There would, however, be a price to pay for our jubilation in meting out our "Apple Orchard Justice." We would all have to listen to Jean lament the loss of a picker and scold us for mistreating him. Fair enough, it was worth every minute because fairness was paramount out here, and cheaters could not be tolerated.

The thumping diesel engine stopped somewhere down the hill for a few minutes, and we all guessed that Randy was giving his rendition of the events that preceded his informal resignation.

When the Boss Lady arrived, sitting atop the tractor, with a red face and teary anger in her eyes, we all knew we were in deep shit.

"Damn you jokers, why can't you be nice to the other kids? Now we are short a man with lots of apples to pick!" she yelled to no one in particular.

Those were the harshest words and the loudest tone I'd ever heard from her. Her eyes watery and her fair skin turned red, she was as mad as I ever wanted to see her. I felt terrible because she was like a mother to all of us and not just our boss, and we were all respectful and protective of her.

Our anger toward Randy was justified: he was cheating the Boss Lady. We tried to ensure the integrity of the tally and weed out a cheat, but in the process, we had hurt the Boss Lady and that felt terrible for all of us. We just stood, with our heads down in shame, as she finished her lamenting the loss of Randy. We didn't know what would happen next. Would she tell George? Would we all get fired? Worst of all for my brothers and me, would she give an unfavorable report to our dad with an ass-whooping to follow?

The Boss Lady was clever, and she took a more subtle approach in the days that followed. She gave us the silent treatment for a few days until she finally gathered us around the tractor before the start of another day.

"Listen up, you jaybirds!" she began, on the following morning. "Since you all act like a bunch of Banti Roosters whenever a new boy shows up to work, I have a surprise for you knuckleheads! We have a college girl starting this afternoon. Her name is Nina, and I want you jokers to be nice to her, capeesh?" We silently looked at each other in stunned amazement, curious to get a glimpse of a real live college chick out here in the dusty orchard with us. Holy shit! A girl picking apples?

Resting up at lunchtime that day, I looked forward to the afternoon push to reach my record setting goal of 200 buckets. I sat in the shade of one of the biggest Gravenstein trees in the orchard, which the Boss Lady said was eighty years old. I thought, man, if I could get to 200 buckets that would sure go a long way toward paying for my school clothes. That's eighteen dollars for only one ten-hour day! As I sat contemplating the possibility of setting a new personal record, the distinct "putt, putt, putt" of a Volkswagen motor sputtered up the gravel driveway, toward the barn and the tired but curious cupcake crew.

An orange VW bug convertible, with the black top down, approached us and we gathered around. Like a pack of wild dogs, we all clamored to get a look at the Berkeley girl. Nina had dirty blonde hair twisted up into a single long ponytail and tied at the end with a small red ribbon. She wore a pair of faded blue jean overalls and white tennis shoes over white ankle socks. She had a nice smile and blue eyes, with a slight build hidden behind her loose fitting overalls. When she spoke, she used perfect, soft English, "Good afternoon, gentlemen, are you waiting for Jean Megini?"

Robbie, being the oldest, replied, "Hi, I'm Robbie, you're in the right place. Jean should be here any minute. You must be Nina?" "Yes, hi Rob, nice to meet you," she said as she extended a hand toward Robbie.

"Hi, I'm Danny and these are my "little" brothers, Richie and John," I interjected after noticing that Nina was kind of cute for an "older" girl, probably eighteen. I emphasized "little" when introducing my brothers and intentionally didn't introduce

Robbie's brother, Perry, so that I would seem more important than the others. Perry homed in and introduced himself right away, not wanting to miss an opportunity to get friendly with a girl. "Hi, I'm Perry," he said. Introductions made, we were curious to see how she would fit in with the cupcake crew.

The Boss Lady arrived, ready for the afternoon, with a couple of plastic jugs filled with refreshing, icy water. She pulled Nina aside and taught her how to fill her bucket with the least amount of effort, beginning with giving her a plastic bucket rather than a heavier metal one, like I used when I first started. We couldn't hear the conversation, but I felt sure that the Boss Lady was warning her about the crew and their propensity for toying with newcomers.

We all watched out of the corner of our eyes and laughed quietly when the "Hippie Girl" picked up the apples, bent over at the knees, a bullseye might as well have been painted on the back of those overalls. We left her alone, however, since the ass chewing that the Boss Lady gave us after Randy quit was still fresh in our minds.

Late in the afternoon, of what had been an uneventful arrival for Nina and the still pensive crew members, we loaded ourselves into the empty bins to go over to another stand of old Gravensteins. Robbie sat on the edge of the front bin with his back toward the Boss Lady, who she sat up in the driver's seat. Nina positioned herself directly across from Robbie in the four-by-four wooden apple bin, and I stood on one side while Richie balanced out the side directly across from me. Off we went through the powdery dust toward our new picking area, slightly bouncing and holding on to the sides of the bin.

I caught Robbie, out of the corner of my eye, trying to discreetly get my attention. He had his left hand around his chin and mouth with his index finger pointing toward Nina as his eyes traveled down her body to a small tear in her overalls. He had spotted the holy grail for young boys, a small, protruding patch of pubic hair!

My heart raced as I spotted the surprise delight and looked back at Robbie with my red face. He just smiled back as we both tried to be as discreet as possible, trying not to stare at the glory patch that had been revealed. This girl picker was going to be interesting, for sure. I think the Boss Lady knew exactly what she was doing.

After a few days, the novelty of the college girl faded into the hot, boring summer, and we started to tease her. We called her "Hippie Girl" and we laughed at her VW bug, since we were all "muscle car" boys.

During lunch break, on her final day as an apple picker, my brother Richie and I piled into the bug with the top down and started in on her. "How long does it take this piece of shit to get up to thirty miles an hour?" I asked. She just smiled and answered in her most polite, correct English, "This car is not a racer, and I like it, so don't call "her" a piece of shit, please."

"Her? So this is a lady bug then?" I said, as I watched Richie rummaging through the glove box. "Get out of there. It's not polite to go through someone else's stuff!" she yelled.

"What are you hiding, Hippie Girl, do you have your weed stashed in there?" I asked. That was enough for her to break out of her polite English as she replied, "Get the fuck out of my car, you little shits!" I don't know if it was the look on her face or the sound of her voice as it broke character, but my brother and

I just started laughing. The harder we laughed, the madder she became, and she finally got out of the car and walked away.

The next morning, she was gone, and the Boss Lady never said a word to us about it. The tongue lashing we were expecting never came and that made us even more nervous.

After a week or so a group of three local girls came to work and managed to last a couple of weeks. The Boss Lady was very protective of them, and we feared retribution from her if we did anything to make them quit. We already had two strikes against us!

I chased one cute young girl, Denise, around under the trees when we were left alone in remote parts of the orchard. I felt her supple, small tight breasts and put my hand down her pants a time or two, and that was the extent of my exploration of the female body at that point in my young life. She was a couple years younger than me, but she seemed to know a lot more about sex than I did, at least in theory.

I learned by doing, by watching her reactions to my touch, and by trial and error. My dad never gave me any information about how to interact with a girl, and the example he set with Mom was horrible. I was on my own, and of course it never crossed my mind to ask Denise for information, because I did the macho thing and pretended to know what I was doing.

Denise and I kind of wrestled around on the ground in the orchard, much like I did with my little brothers but with a twist. She had nice soft bumps on her chest, and she smelled much nicer than my brothers, even in the hot, salty sweat of the summer orchard dust. She egged me on by teasing and talking nasty to me, but then she put up a pseudo-fight when I started to touch her. Thus began my confusion in the ways of women that still confound me today.

Toward the end of summer, the Boss Lady drove down Burnside Road from her house up on Darby Road, and spotted Denise and I rolling around under the apple trees. She came up into the orchard on her tractor and when she reached us, she just smiled and commented, "Sure looked like you two were really fighting for the same apples there for a minute!" Denise and I blushed and acted like nothing had happened but we knew she was on to us.

The summer was over and school would be starting after the Labor Day weekend. Our crew disbanded and we went our separate ways.

We had each made some money for school clothes while learning the benefits and routine of hard work. The harder you worked, the more money you made; it was a simple and effective system. The lazy kids made less than the hard workers and that seemed fair. The group weeded out cheaters and the core crew formed a bond through our common purpose.

We were all loyal and respectful to the Boss Lady, who was not just our boss but our teacher. She looked after us and gave us some valuable life lessons along the way, encouraged us to save a little money if we could, and to be tolerant and fair with each other. She gave us an understanding of teamwork.

Boss Lady Jean was like the patient, tolerant mother I didn't have at home, and a hard-working woman who cared about people. I feel honored to have had her as a critical part of my youth when I was developing my values and character, and she will never be forgotten.

Gramps Cottage

BACK HOME, I WAS BEING taught other lessons in life by my dad, both in deed and word, lots and lots of words, spoken with volume and conviction, as if my very life depended on it.

My dad was a five foot seven, 140-pound, pissed-off SOB with a Napoleon complex, complete with a loud and frightening presence, learned most likely from his drill sergeant in the U.S. Marine Corps during his late teen years in the Korean War. I was taught to pay attention, do as I was told without question, and to stuff my feelings deep down into my gut, never allowing them to be expressed. If I was unfortunate enough to enter the house in the afternoon, when he was back from a bar and freshly drunk, that usually meant a couple hours of loud, rambling lectures at the kitchen table. I felt like a scared, trapped animal. He would barrage me often with conflicting life directives and lessons. When I hear people say they would rather be physically assaulted quickly than be subject to rambling, emotional abuse, I know exactly what they mean. He spoke with an urgency and authority that made it hard to take as a boy but take it I did. What choice did I have in the matter?

"You're smarter than the rest, Danny, and you need to be! The small guys like us have to always think one step ahead; we have to be quick and fearless, you have to outsmart the big, dumb, and slow guys, because physically they will crush you if you give them the chance!" Dad's lectures prepared me for conflict and battle and were, unfortunately, short on compassion and the importance of human relationships. "Ninety-nine percent of the world is made up of assholes that couldn't find their own ass with both hands!" He continued, "You're smarter than that, you can be anything you want, don't let people tell you any different . . . ." He droned on and on while I nodded occasionally. When the tone sharpened and grew louder, punctuated by "Do you understand me?" I replied with a simple, "Yes, Dad."

The "Billy D. Lectures," as I call them, included musings and worldly advice on such diverse topics as women ("Women are like streetcars. If you miss this one, there will be another one coming along in about ten minutes."); God and heaven ("When you're dead, you're dead, and that's a long time!") and ("Mother Nature is the most powerful God there is. Those people down at the Church on Sundays don't have a clue; they just believe what some preacher tells them to believe because they are too dumb and lazy to figure it out for themselves!"); family ("Family is all you've got, so take care of them."); and keeping up with the Joneses ("I don't give a shit what your friends' parents do or have! Be lucky you have a roof over your head, a warm place to sleep, and a hot meal once in a while!"). Since I was the oldest son, it was my responsibility to listen to these lectures and prepare myself for taking care of the family when he was gone, which in his mind wouldn't be long. Hell, I was only twelve years old! I just wanted to be a kid and play ball, have fun with my friends, do what the other kids did.

I could feel a growing, painful knot in my stomach during these lectures, a feeling of fear tied up inside me, a desire to run away from the unpredictability of a fearful man who had captured me and was now toying with me like a mouse in a corner. Adrenaline, flight or fight, with nowhere to go but down and into my gut, tearing away like acid, the feeling burned within me from the inside out.

Sweating, squirming, glued to the vinyl padded kitchen chair with no escape, an internal panic arose that I dare not reveal to my captor, lest he pounce on me in full fury. He sat at the head of the table, smoking a non-filter Camel cigarette and sipping on a Coors from the yellow pop-top can, as he delivered his crazy take on life. I had absolutely no choice but to endure this torture, without facial expression, question, or argument, knowing that any such response would fuel his anger and lengthen the encounter. Helpless and afraid, mentally and emotionally exhausted, embarrassed, and angry, I sat and waited for an end to the madness.

What would my friends think? My schoolteachers? My football and Little League coaches? The classmates at Twin Hills who thought I was so smart and funny? What would everyone think if they knew the true story of my family? Nobody would ever know, nobody could ever know, or the illusion would be shattered, and I would be shattered and destroyed, so thought my twelve-year-old self. Better to just sit and be quiet, pretend I have a "normal" family. I hid my shame and embarrassment from the world, protected the family secret, took on the burden, and kept up the illusion of normalcy as best I could.

However, there was one lifeline of sanity within my grasp: The detached little cottage, workshop, radio room, and TV repair shop where Gramps lived off and on between his stints at the VA Hospital.

Gramps never raised his voice and never spoke ill of anybody. He didn't understand why my dad was so angry all the time, or why he yelled at full volume.

Gramps had created a radio room in the back section of the cottage. He would sit patiently and write down translations of the da-dit-dit-da's of Morse code coming in from ships all around the world. He taught me how to send code on the little double black button attached to a lever with a set of points that sends the signal into the wires. Dit-dit-dit dah-dah-dah dit-dit-dit translates to SOS or Save Our Ship.

Gramps made the best of his situation and felt lucky to have a place among family, a place to work his daily crossword puzzles and to fix radios and televisions in the little workshop. He told old Navy war stories to his grandkids and enjoyed his last precious breaths of life from the cool morning air of the apple orchard. He loved to go on camping and fishing trips to the Russian River or up to Clearlake to fish for big catfish at Rodman Slough, where he felt like he was a boy again, back in Arkansas. He was always there to listen to us or to just hang out when I didn't want to go into the main house with Dad, who was often looking for someone to punish for crimes real or imagined.

Gramps had lung cancer and breathed with his one remaining lung while still smoking cigarettes and having coughing spells. He never complained or said an angry word to anyone. He was the polar opposite of my loud, angry father and a welcome calming presence. His cottage had a bed, heater, couch, and a small table where the radio sat. Alongside an ashtray was his yellow tin of Topps tobacco. Although the room often had a thick smell of cigarettes, I loved to hang out there and listen to Gramps tell stories of WWII in the South Pacific and of his bootleg-whiskey running days back in Arkansas.

Despite having only one lung left and his constant shortness of breath, he would occasionally break out his harmonica and play for me and my brothers. Next to his bed, on the wooden floor, was always a makeshift spittoon—a Folger's coffee can. Slimy, stinky, and with a consistency of olive oil, he would occasionally ask me to dump it outside in the orchard. I would return it to his bedside, empty and rinsed out with water, where it would be refilled by the near constant fluid buildup in his single remaining lung.

On one otherwise uneventful visit to his cottage, Richie and I were playing grab ass around that side of the bed and knocked over the nearly full spit can. Out spilled the vile and disgusting fluid, made more so by the swollen, extinguished cigarette butts that splashed across the floor, under the bed, and along the wall. Richie and I looked at each other, each blaming the other, while Gramps just gently told us both to clean it up. Wiping that mess up with towels was one of the most disgusting tasks I have ever done. I nearly vomited! Once the mess was cleaned to Gramps' satisfaction he simply said, "Next time you boys just go outside and fight, not in here, OK?" To which we both agreed. That was Gramps; he didn't get violently upset, he didn't get physical, yell, or blame; no, Gramps simply accepted what the situation was and took prudent action without complaint or anger. I found it hard to believe that my father's father could be so vastly different in temperament!

When Gramps was gone, the cottage was sometimes used as an overnight flop house for one of Dad's drunken buddies. On one Saturday morning, my brothers and I quietly peeked in through the door to see a ball of snoring blankets on the floor and a detached prosthetic leg several feet away. We giggled at the sight and watched as the groggy man awoke slowly and emerged from the blankets and looked around.

My sister, Debbie, was off somewhere with her stoner boyfriend as usual, and that was just fine with me because I never really bonded with her; in fact, I had arguments with her about why motorcycles were better than her transportation of choice, horses. I didn't have a motorcycle, but I envied the Alberdingi boys up the street when they walked home after school and immediately took turns spitting dust out behind their Honda 70. on the orchard road next to the bus lanes at Twin Hills School. I was interested in sports and Debbie hated the jocks at school, gravitating instead to the stoner crowd. I suppose she just needed what we all need—acceptance and people to relate to without judgment. I was embarrassed by her and her choice of friends, her pot smoking, and her "I don't give a shit" attitude. She and my brothers and I were adversaries, sharing a household terribly short on money, love, compassion, and comfort. We each had to develop survival skills and fit in where we could while trying to maintain the façade of being part of a "normal" family.

The groggy man in the ball of blankets searching for his missing leg turned out to be a fellow Korean War veteran. Dad had brought him in the night before because he was too drunk to drive home, and he didn't want to face his wife. Dad told this to Mom as he cooked his buddy "Jim" some fresh eggs that I had to go find out around the barn in one of the random free-range nests.

I ran out and told the still groggy and disoriented man that Dad was cooking him some breakfast and he'd be out in a few minutes. Since Dad never cooked breakfast for us, I thought Jim should and would be delighted, but he was not gracious nor appreciative. "Fuck breakfast, I just want a ride home!" Jim replied angrily as he fastened his wooden leg.

Normally respectful, I surprised myself by blurting out, "You're an asshole. He's cooking breakfast for you!" I knew my remark was a huge mistake as I watched Jim hop up the two steps onto the deck and into the kitchen with an angry look on his face. "Danny, get your ass in here right now!" Dad yelled out the back door. I took a deep breath and walked into the kitchen to face his wrath. I knew I'd made a mistake and that the punishment would be brutal and instantaneous.

He asked if it was true what I'd called his buddy to which I replied, "Yes, but I didn't mean to, it just came out." As he took his belt off and doubled it over in his hands, he said to me, "Apologize to Mr. Jim!" I did as I was told, and Jim just smirked at me.

The blows from the belt came hard and fast, stinging my arm, back, and butt while Dad yelled, "You don't ever disrespect an adult like that! You know better than that!" I cried and whimpered and tried to slow the stinging blows by putting my arms in the way, but it was little help. Finally, he stopped, but as if putting on a show for his buddy, he added, "Every time I hear you stop crying, I'm gonna come back in and whip your disrespectful little ass again!" He closed the bedroom door behind him and returned to the kitchen.

I moaned and cried for a while, and when I stopped the door opened and the belt started swinging again. I hurt, cried, and yelped. Back out to the kitchen he went leaving me crying on the floor of my bedroom again.

I was trapped, hurt, angry, and afraid. Hoping Dad would just stop, I thought to myself, "Please just eat and take your friend home." As I sat crying, I heard the phone ring and Dad answered. The call was from the emergency room at Palm Drive Hospital. Several minutes into the conversation, I could gather that Debbie had been shot point blank in the stomach and was in critical condition. At that moment all I could think was, "Thank God, now he'll have to stop hitting me and go to the hospital!"

Many years later, I cry a deep and lonely sadness for the loss of sibling relationships, living in a house of survival and fear, everyone watching out for themselves by necessity. The shame that my first thought, when hearing that my fourteen-year-old sister was shot, was a self-centered one lives with me to this day.

I blame the tyranny of an alcoholic father who created an environment where siblings couldn't love and support one another nor feel proud, free, and happy. I cry for my sister who never knew a loving, caring father who protected and guided her into healthy adulthood. I cry a deep and aching cry for my two little brothers and for myself who never developed a deep love for one another. These tears cleanse my soul and give me the strength to teach my children and grandchildren the value of love that a family can share. I can pave the way for a better understanding by sharing my experience, and I can now forgive my father and myself.

Today, I am able to release the shame and tell my brothers and sister that I love them; although there is no going back, no changing what was, there is only living each day in gratitude and hope. That is enough, to know that I did the hard work and changed a long-standing family pattern. I broke the binding chains of a destructive family cycle and continue to do so one day at a time.

It has been a long and slow process, spanning many years, to pull myself up and out of a family legacy of fear and self-destruction to become vulnerable enough to love and accept my family for who they are without judgment.

How could a young boy process a life where his sister, by all estimations and expectations, probably wouldn't live to see her seventeenth birthday and yet somehow managed to survive? Hitchhiking across the U.S., from California to New York, alone at fourteen years old, not once, but twice! Accidentally shot at point blank with a .22 pistol by a boyfriend and survive the nine bullet holes as the shot passed through her coiled up intestines. Or jumping from a moving car after hitching a ride with a psycho and breaking her perfectly straight teeth, paid for with the only money for braces that our family ever had to spend on such a luxury.

Living on the road as a carny, working at carnivals across the country. Skidding down the middle of River Road, after the biker she was sitting behind laid it down when his Harley broke apart. Stints in various hospitals and jails, yellow as a banana with hepatitis from sharing dope needles and other experiences of self-destructive behavior, all in service of finding some semblance of love and acceptance from anyone, anywhere.

Yes, sister Debbie was, and is, a fearless survivor, and I bore witness to the depths to which a lack of love could take her. I wondered and worried as a young buy, would she make it out of those desperately horrid conditions to find her way in the world? I prayed that she could and would, somehow, some way.

I looked for happier things to focus upon and developed a I love of music. I had a small plastic radio at my bedside that I kept tuned to 610AM KFRC in San Francisco and the "Dr. Donald D. Rose Show," where he played all of "today's top hits!"

I prided myself on learning all the names and melodies of the songs. There was a TV show called "Name That Tune" where the host would give the contestants a short description of a song and they would say, "I can name that tune in four notes," or three or one as the challenge played out. I always thought I could have won if I were only ten years older.

The Archies' "Sugar, Sugar" was a snappy little tune from 1969 that I liked, along with all the hip songs like "Satisfaction" by the Rolling Stones and "Cal Commotion" by Creedence Clearwater Revival, and Stevie Wonders' "Superstitious" in 1973. Of course, the Beatles were the best, and I loved to sing all of their songs from "Hard Day's Night" to "Lucy in the Sky with Diamonds."

Music was always on, but I loved to watch *The Partridge Family* on TV every week, especially the guitar player, a young, red-headed freckle-faced boy named Danny. All the young girls were in love with David Cassidy! I played the drums in school band, so I learned to keep a good beat and appreciate music.

Cosmo, the drummer for Creedence Clearwater Revival, was my hero, along with Ringo from the Beatles. I distinctly remember sitting on an old couch on our front porch with my friend

Mark Lewis and just matter-of-factly deciding to write a few songs as it were that easy. I mean, how hard could it be if Hank Williams could wring such a big hit out of singing "Hey, Good Lookin', Whatcha got Cookin'?" I liked to play with words and rhymes, patching together meanings and ideas in different ways. It was fun and free!

I once fancied myself a disc jockey when I was about ten or eleven years old. My dad was the chief engineer of Santa Rosa radio station KSRO, "1350 on your dial, Santa Rosa style," as their slogan went.

As the oldest boy in our family, I endured the painful kitchen table lectures and the 2:30 a.m. wake-up calls to go fishing in the stormiest weather. I was taught to be responsible for everything—and everyone in the family. The burden was large for a pre-teen boy but, on the other hand, I was the one who got to go to work at the radio station with Dad.

The emergency broadcast station and antenna on Stony Point Road sat out in a large field where wild pheasants and deer roamed. The small brick building and antenna didn't look like much, but the radio transmitter was the heart of the radio station..

Dad would come here whenever the station inadvertently went "off the air" due to some technical difficulty. Any such outage was immediately known in our house, because the 1936 Packard-Bell radio on top of the refrigerator was always on and exclusively tuned to 1350 AM KSRO.

The main broadcasting station was located on the east side of Santa Rosa, on the second floor of the Flamingo Hotel. Complete with a conference center, large pool, restaurant, and bar, the Flamingo was a swank place back in the day.

The extra interview studio, surrounded by soundproof glass, was my play place. I sat between the two turntables made to "spin" 45 rpm singles or 33 rpm vinyl record albums. A large headphone set nearly covered my eleven-year-old head as I looked at an array of dials, lights, and meters behind a flexible microphone. Dad gave me free rein to act like Wolfman Jack. The walls from floor to ceiling were filled with 45s and albums. I asked Dad for the Beatles *Help* album for my birthday, and he pulled it off the shelf and gave it to me.

Outside of my dream radio station and several feet away was the live studio where Dad, much to his dismay, had to occasionally DJ and read the news. Although he was the chief engineer who kept the transmitter equipment in proper working order, KSRO was a small radio station with limited staff. This required him to DJ.

On one memorable occasion I joined him in the live studio and watched as he prepared for and then proceeded to read the news, live on the air, that he had pulled from a teletype machine out in the hallway. The turntable was cued up with a 33 rpm album. Once he finished reading the news, he started the turntable and shut off his microphone. Iron Butterfly's "In-A-Gadda-Da-Vida" started playing.

The 33 rpm spun as the record player's needle worked its way from the outside diameter down toward the center of the black vinyl record. The seventeen-minute song went on and on. I watched the needle approach the halfway point and thought to myself, "Oh no, what if Dad doesn't make it back before the song ends?!" I readied myself for this possibility by looking at the 45 rpm record on the second turntable on the DJ console, the much tamer tune "Joy to the World" by Three Dog Night, which was cued up and ready to go.

I had it drilled into my head that *I* was responsible for everything within my awareness and that meant doing what I could to save Dad. Would he get fired if he didn't perform his DJ duties properly? If I didn't do something, would it be my fault? Was Dad testing me to see if I could perform in an emergency?

Just as I was rehearsing what I was going to say on air, the song ended and in walked Dad with the smell of bourbon on his breath.

Apparently, this wasn't the first time his cocktail break was facilitated by a long version of a song. I didn't realize that the song was also playing down in the Flamingo Bar and that Dad had the timing down perfectly. I was much relieved that I didn't have to put my nervous preparation into practice!

The surrounding valleys at home were filled with electric guitar music. Hippies moved up from San Francisco after the 1967 Summer of Love turned into a crazy scene. They camped out in old barns and abandoned chicken coops throughout the western Sonoma County countryside. The communes—Morningstar Ranch a few miles away on Graton Road and then the Wheeler Ranch out on Coleman Valley Road, just west of Occidental, were attracting flower children too.

Somehow, we ended up with two hippie draft dodgers seeking refuge in Gramps' cottage while he was back for an extended stay at the VA hospital. Dale and Cecil became Beany and Cecil when we renamed them after the then popular kid's TV puppet show. I guess my hardcore U.S. Marine Dad had become sympathetic to these young men who were being forced to ship off to Vietnam and die for our country. I was always told that hippies were lazy, longhaired freaks who were on drugs all the time, but my experience with Dale and Cecil provided a very different view.

Dale was clean shaven, except for his well-groomed lamb chop sideburns. He had straight, brown hair cut below the ears in the style of the Beatles and looked like he could have been in a hippy-love-groove band at the time. He was quiet and agreeable, and he seemed happy to just be out in the country here with his buddy Cecil.

Cecil had long and unruly frizzy black hair that he tied into a ponytail and equally unruly, random patches of hair growing out of his face. He was boisterous and outgoing, loved to play kid games with us, and being tall and thin, he was a ball of energy as well. Cecil smiled a lot, his haphazard teeth gleamed in the sunshine. They put up tie-dyed cloth for curtains in the cottage and burned incense as Cecil played his electric guitar and Dale sang and rattled his tambourine.

We added an extra leaf to the yellow vinyl-topped kitchen table so they could eat dinner with us. The myth of the lazy hippy was debunked for me when Dale and Cecil spent several days building a chicken pen out behind the barn. The pen was complete with a watering system and was raccoon and fox proof, along with two sturdy roosts with narrow ladders for the chickens to walk up at night. They built six nesting boxes and filled them with hay so we could easily gather the eggs. All of this was made of scrap lumber gathered up around the big red barn, and it turned out beautiful!

The calming and fun presence of the two hippies was evident one evening as we all sat around the table after dinner to celebrate brother Richie's eighth birthday with a freshly made birthday cake. We all donned our pointy party hats, including Dale and Cecil. The hippies made us all laugh as they looked and acted like the rest of us kids, Cecil blowing into his party horn and Dale watching and laughing as it uncurled and recoiled while making the squeaky duck call noises. We all joyfully sang, "Happy birthday, dear Richie" as he blew out the eight flaming candles with a big smile on his face.

Most weekends the sound of screaming electric guitars and drumbeats reverberated throughout the valley to the south and west. The Beatles were the impetus for youngsters everywhere to pick up a guitar and just play and play, which they did. I loved the sounds and the excitement of music and made it part ofmy daily life at an early age.

I learned to keep a steady beat from playing the drums at Twin Hills school. Records and record stores were seemingly everywhere, even Analy Rexall and Fiesta Pharmacies had great record album sections in their stores. I loved to go in and browse the alphabetically arranged full-sized albums, complete with cover art and photos of the band members.

In 1973, a new music store opened on Main Street called People's Music. I loved to go in and look at the rows of guitars hung along the walls and the full drum sets assembled out on the floor among many other types and sizes of musical instruments that I had never seen before.

My grade buddies, Brad, Gardner, David, and I decided, at the last minute, to enter the talent show at school. We decided to lip/instrument sync Jimi Hendrix's song, "Purple Haze." We had a complete drum set, courtesy of the Twin Hills Band, but no other instruments. We marched down to Peoples' Music and matter-of-factly asked if we could borrow a bass guitar and an electric guitar for the talent show. The proprietor said cheer-fully, "Sure thing boys, just bring 'em back when you're finished with your show!" Just like that—no contracts, no signatures, just small-town trust. We were a hit and promptly returned the instruments the very next day with a big "thank you."

The album section at People's Music was spectacular, and I spent what seemed like hours looking at them. Some of my favorite covers were the Beatles' *Yellow Submarine* album with its cartoon art, the red, white, and blue flag thumbprint on Don McLean's *American Pie* (one of my all-time favorite songs), and the cover for the Beatles' *Sgt. Pepper's Lonely Hearts Club Band,* with its intricate, semi-hidden mixture of faces and objects. Pink Floyd's *Dark Side of the Moon* with the prism breaking white light into a rainbow of colors was cool and Led Zeppelin's *Houses of the Holy,* which featured naked children climbing up a rocky hill, was shocking at the time for me. Showing a naked butt on a record cover?!

Despite warnings from my mom to stay away from "those creeps" and the smell of Patchouli oil, which I mistook for the smell of marijuana while walking in downtown Sebastopol, I found the hippies to be colorful, happy, and friendly. Sure, some were short on personal hygiene but so what.

On walks downtown, I liked a hippie store located in an old building sandwiched between the Atlantic Richfield gas station and the Analy Theater on Main Street. Upstairs was a small room with walls entirely filled with Blacklight Posters. When you closed the door behind you, it took a minute for your eyes to adjust to the eerie semi-darkness and the vibrant reflected col-ors from the posters and on your own white shirt and shoelaces. I thought that was the coolest thing, while at the same time I wondered if this is how the hippies saw the world all the time, even out in the sun when they smoked that stinky weed or ate LSD? Although I loved the colors, I was very afraid to even consider any kind of drug or other weird stuff. We had a plant that grew all over the apple orchard called jimson weed and the pods would dry out in the summer and open to reveal small black seeds. Apparently, some hippies smoked the seeds and freaked out as if being on an LSD acid trip and ended up in the hospital.

Just as suddenly and unexpectedly as they had appeared, our hippies were up and gone in one day. Dad said they were going to visit friends in Canada. I was sad when they left, as they were fun, playful, and colorful guys and became a part of our family, even if only for a couple months. I think Dad accommodated to the young men because he understood the horrors of war and the tremendous sacrifice, for what seemed like nothing but a pat on the back and a kick in the ass, after fighting someone else's war halfway across the world.

Liar, Liar, Pants on Fire!

WE LOADED UP THE OLD 1959 Rambler station wagon with the camping boxes—wooden apple lug boxes packed with just about anything you might need for camping and fishing: canned beans, corned beef hash, Vienna sausages, tuna, and small cardboard containers of beef and chicken bouillon cubes; the quintessential Dutch oven, cast iron frying pans, plates, forks, knives, spoons, a spatula, a can opener, dishwashing soap and scrubbers, a percolator and a can of Folgers ground coffee, aluminum foil, freezer and garbage bags, paper towels, toilet paper, hand soap, and drying towels; a first aid kit, extra fishing hooks in various sizes, sinkers and spools of fishing line, swivels and leader hardware, needle-nose pliers, filet knives, and duct tape. A separate box contained the Coleman lantern and fuel, plus extra packages of mantles. The contents of the camping boxes had been assembled by Dad over several years of camping trips and after each one asking, "What did we forget? What did we need that we didn't bring? What would have made the trip more enjoyable?"

After sliding the boxes, ice chest, and a plastic, five-gallon water jug into the back of the Rambler, the blue tarps, sleeping bags, and a spool of light rope went on top while the fishing poles were placed carefully on the sides. An old, well-used greasy cooking grill, wrapped in old newspaper, was slid in alongside the fishing poles. Extra jackets, shoes, socks, and a few snacks completed our supplies. We were ready to roll toward our camping adventure.

It was the previous year, when I was just 12 years old, that I learned to drive this old Rambler. I had to sit on a pillow to see over the dash, as my legs were just barely long enough to reach the peddles. My left leg struggled to depress the clutch when shifting gears on the column three speed, a.k.a. "Three on the tree!"

We looked like a carload of Okies from the *Grapes of Wrath,* and being in no big hurry to get anywhere, we pulled over occasionally to let cars pass. That was Dad's way. He didn't care what anyone thought, where or how fast they were going. He and Gramps would just say, "Good luck, hope you make it" or "Where's the fire?"

That day we stayed closer to home and went to our favorite place on the lower Russian River, a fishing spot about a mile inland from where the river meets the cold and windy ocean at Jenner. Dad drove while Gramps rode shotgun. My brothers, Richie and John, sat in the back seat next to me among the pile of sleeping bags and jackets. With a cold can of Olympia Beer between Dad's legs and one in Gramps' hand, we were on our way. A few miles into our journey, Dad flicked the ashes off his Camel out the front window, and they immediately blew back into my face. I dared not complain and just watched for the occasional wrist flick, so I could close my eyes for a second when the ashes flew back in my face.

The drive out to the Russian River was a slow and scenic twenty-mile journey. We traveled west on Bodega Highway, past the little yellow Spring Hill store and gas station and then slowly up O'Farrell Hill as the old Rambler sputtered and pulled. Eventually we headed down into the tiny town of Freestone. The Bohemian Highway starts at Freestone, where the only establishment of note was Rocco's Store—a gas, bar, and BBQ burger joint. We followed the narrow and winding Bohemian Highway through the thickening stands of redwood trees to Occidental. The loaded Rambler puttered slowly along through the small town, past the mainstays of Italian family-style dining—Negri's on the left and the Union Hotel and Fiori's Restaurant on the right. Gonnella's Country Mart and the Panizzera Meat Shop added to the not so subtle announcement that this was an Italian Village. The redwood trees thickened along Dutch Bill Creek as we wound our way past Camp Meeker, where the creek was usually dammed up in the summer for swimmers. The dam had been taken down for the winter, so the creek flowed freely through the forests along the highway. The post office was a little trailer painted dark blue and flanked by community bulletin boards. We were approaching "hippy territory," where long-haired, bearded men with tie-dyed T-shirts were a common sight. Many parts of the Bohemian Highway stayed wet for months, since the winter sun had no chance of penetrating the vast redwood canopy.

Out past the "Closed for Winter" summer camps, where the parking lots were littered with brown pine needles and fallen dark-green redwood branches, we drove by the small Monte Rio

Elementary School and rounded the last curve of the highway. The Pink Elephant bar on the right and Bartlett's Market on the left welcomed us to Monte Rio and the Russian River. I strained to get a look at the flowing river as we went across the green metal bridge that crossed over to Highway 116, where the old Quonset hut-style Rio Theater stood on the corner.

We followed Highway 116, with the downstream flow along the Russian River, toward the ocean. Sunlight flickered in and out of the Rambler's windows as the redwood trees allowed flecks of sunlight through. The general store at Duncans Mills was a big, wooden-floored building, straight out of an old Western movie. They had a little bit of everything on the shelves and certainly the few essentials Dad needed. He came out with a case of Olympia Beer, a bag of ice, a couple packs of smokes, and a brown paper bag concealing a jug of cheap wine for Gramps. He must have talked Mom out of a few extra bucks that morning, because after he loaded the beer and ice into the ice chest, he pulled out a small bag of beef jerky and tossed it to me in the back seat saying, "Here, share that with your brothers."

Just a few short miles down the road we reached our spot on the river. I was still clutching the unopened bag of jerky while Richie and John pestered me for their share. Dad steered the old Rambler gently off the road and into a clearing of flat gravelly beach along the river. Tall blackberry bushes, with waxy looking red and green poison oak leaves mixed in, separated our private little beach spot from Highway 116. The river took a wide bend where a large rocky mountain redirected its course and created a calm, deep cove. Upstream from the cove, about twenty yards or so, there was a small seasonal creek that flowed into the river. The creek had, over time, carved its way down and underneath the highway to the river, which was located in a wide gravel canyon surrounded by tall willow trees. Where the cold, rapid creek met the river was the sweet spot for trout fishing. The willow branches provided anchor points for our blue tarps if it rained, while the canyon itself shielded us from the wind during the night as we slept.

The beach was littered with dead branches, perfect for firewood. Gathering firewood was always the first chore for my brothers and me. Firewood, firewood, stacks of firewood, to feed the fire that would never go out until the day we left. Once the stack of firewood was placed on the beach in front of the Rambler, Richie, John, and I walked back to the sheltered canyon of the little creek, carefully down a narrow trail through willow branches, where we spread out the blue plastic tarp on the ground. The tarp would be the only barrier between our sleeping bags and the cold, hard gravel.

After a few trips from the Rambler down to the creek, our sleeping bags and gear in place, it was time for some fishing. Dad and Gramps had the fire going about ten yards in front of the Rambler, downstream from the sleepy canyon along the rocky beach. Dad purposefully fed wood into the fire while Gramps positioned his folding chair a few yards away. Dad taught me how important a fire was to provide heat for cooking and warmth, light to see by, and to keep wild animals away at night. Fire has a hypnotic effect that goes back to caveman times. Oral history has passed down through generations, while circling a fire, by indigenous peoples around the World dating back thousands of years.

As we approached the warm, crackling campfire, fishing poles in hand, Dad yelled out, "This wood pile isn't going to last twenty minutes! Put those poles down and keep bringing wood!"

Just as we were walking past the fire and down the gravelly beach to look for more wood, in drove a familiar pickup truck. It was Gramps' old wino buddy, Harry, with his stepson, Donald. Harry got out of his copper-colored 1956 Ford with a brown paper sack and headed toward the fire.

My brothers and I greeted Donald and encouraged his help in finding more firewood. "Come on 'Kunt,' we need more firewood!" I chided him right away. Donald ran after me, threatening to punch me if I called him Kunt again. I couldn't help that his last name was Kendt! The little chase worked out perfectly, because when he gave up we were standing next to loads of dead pine branches, perfect for firewood. Donald was a year older than me and had picked apples with us the previous summer, but he wasn't particularly bright or athletic. "OK, Donald, I won't call you Kunt anymore!" I said, emphasizing the word Kunt. "Grab those two big logs there," I added, pointing toward a short covering of berry and poison oak vines, "and I'll take this long one," as I grabbed a dry branch from the clearing under the rotting tree. Richie and John laughed to themselves as Donald reached into the glistening, oily red, poison oak leaves to retrieve the logs. My brothers knew only too well the itchy misery that awaited him tomorrow. We had learned the hard way, after many camping trips, that poison oak was no joke.

Once we had built up the firewood pile, I grabbed my fishing pole, ready to get down to business. I held a coffee can full of red worms that I had dug up back at home, out behind the barn. After only a couple of shovel scoops in the rich loam soil of the apple orchard, I had several dozen nicely sized worms for fishing. I baited my hook with what I hoped the trout would see as one of the irresistible, little squirmers before handing over the can to Richie. "Here, you dogs go downstream and find your own spot. I'm going upstream."

Once back at the sweet spot, where cold creek water mixed into the slow churning river, I surveyed the water. I imagined the curious and hungry little trout pointed toward the creek outlet, patiently waiting for the current to wash down a bug, fly, or my juicy worm. I noticed the speed, color, and ripple effects of the water flow and picked what I thought was the most promising spot. A nice cast, with a well-practiced arc, and my baited hook and sinker splashed down on target, ten feet out into the river. I reeled up the slack as my pulse quickened, and the nerves in my arm, hands, and fingers tingled with heightened sensitivity and anticipation. I was alert for any small and quick "tick" on the line that would signal a nibble. Quiet and still, holding my breath as long as possible so I wouldn't miss the slightest movement, I stood patiently on the riverbank, alert and ready.

But it was midday and the fish had no interest in lunch; in fact, they pretty much only eat at dawn and dusk, but I was so excited that I had to try anyway. I gave up after a half hour of breath control and silence before walking back down the beach, past the fire where Dad, Gramps, and Harry sat sipping wine and beer, fully engaged in a good old-fashioned bullshitting session. I continued on down to where Kunt and my brothers were screwing around and trying to fish. I arrived just in time to see John forget to release the thumb button on his reel as he swung his fishing rod in an arc toward the water. His sinker splashed down hard only a few feet in front of him. With their lines in the water, Richie and Kunt were playing grab ass but not really paying attention. "You dipshits have probably scared away any fish, with all the noise you're making down here!" I teased. "John, you need to put a new worm on your hook! With a cast like that, that worm probably flew clear across the river when the sinker hit the water!" I said as I grabbed the can of worms to help him.

The sun started going down and the bugs gathered as I headed quietly back to my sweet spot where the creek entered the river. Once there, I cast out a fresh worm and tightened up the slack while my senses readjusted to maximum sensitivity. As the sunlight began to dissipate, I could barely see where my fishing line entered the water, but I didn't really need to see anyway, as this was all about feel. Boom! There it was—a quick hit. I could feel the struggle of a strong but panicked little trout, hooked on the end of my line. As the tip of my fishing pole bent down toward the water, I set the hook by quickly jerking the pole upward. Feeling the struggling fish excited me as I slowly reeled it in. Keeping the line tight, the fighting trout darted left, then right, in an attempt to escape. I landed the little pan fryer up onto the gravelly bank, quickly grabbed my prize, and put it on the stringer that I'd retrieved from my pocket. Looking around and back down toward the campfire to see if anyone had seen me catch the trout, I was relieved the short struggle had not caught the attention of Kunt and my brothers, because they would surely run down here to fish and ruin my spot! I landed three more shiny trout before it got too dark to see and walked back to the fire with what I knew was going to be a tasty dinner.

Everyone was back around the fire now, that constant source of light and heat, the focal point and social center of every camping trip. Holding my fishing pole with my right hand, I raised my left hand and held up my bounty: four fresh trout, each about eight inches long. "Look what I caught!" I said proudly. My brothers and Kunt looked at my catch in amazement and envy. Dad, Harry, and Gramps looked up, as I interrupted their bullshit session, and Dad said, "Damn nice of you to catch some dinner for us, Danny!" He continued, "Go get the big cast iron skillet, that can of cooking oil, a bowl, and a package of crackers out of the Rambler, and bring 'em back here. Oh, and grab two eggs out of the cooler and that brown paper bag that's in the front seat!" I put down the stringer of fish on the gravel and did as I was told.

I returned to the fire with the cooking supplies just as Dad lit the mantle on the Coleman lantern and hung it on a willow branch. He put the skillet on the edge of the campfire and immediately gutted the trout and tossed the small spoonful of guts into the river. "Break the eggs into that bowl and scramble them up," he ordered. I did as I was told and prepared to hand him the bowl. "Donald don't just sit there with your thumb up your ass! Crush up the crackers in that brown paper bag!" Kunt snapped to it and had a bag half full of crushed Ritz in no time. All of us watched as Dad poured a little cooking oil into the now hot frying pan. He took each of the fresh trout, one by one, and dipped them into the eggs, put them into the bag of cracker crumbs and shook them, then placed them into the hot pan. The sizzling trout soon emitted a savory aroma that made my stomach rumble. I watched them darken in the hot oil as smoke carried that wonderful smell upward.

Dad placed the first one onto a stainless-steel plate with a stamped "USMC 1944" on the underside and said, as he handed it to me, "Give that one to your Grandfather!" I did as I was told and Gramps happily took the plate from me and said, "Thank you, Danny. You're one hell of a fisherman!" The next plate went to Harry, and the third one, Dad said, was mine because I caught them. Dad kept the last one as he pulled the frying pan out and away from the fire and said to Kunt and my brothers, "Go over there in the camping box and grab a couple cans of Spam and a can of pork and beans." All three of them looked dejected, but they did as they were ordered and without complaint. "Maybe tomorrow you boys will fish instead of screwing around, but tonight it's Spam and beans!" I dared not laugh or smirk, but I was thinking, "Yeah, you dipshits, trout for me and Spam for you lame suckers, ha ha!"

The darkness brought cold, almost freezing, air to the shore of the river. Dad, Gramps, and Harry kept warm with alcohol and a close proximity to the campfire, while the rest of us stood around the fire and turned our bodies around like vertical rotisseries, standing as close as we could get to the warmth. Half of my body was freezing while the other half got almost too hot, hence the constant turning around every few minutes. There is something ancient and comforting about hovering around a fire, staring into the everchanging flames while basking in its warmth and light. Gramps and Harry, seated in folding camp chairs, bantered back and forth while under the influence of a shared jug of Burgundy wine. Dad stood and droned on about one of his survival stories as a marine during the Korean War. Something about basic training and parachuting into the high treetops of the Okeefenokee Swamp, eating bugs to survive while avoiding the alligators below.

We had just settled in around the fire and its hypnotizing warmth when suddenly and without warning flames started climbing up the back leg of Richie's pants. I was directly across the fire, alongside John and Kunt, facing the flames, and I couldn't believe what I was seeing! We looked on as Richie didn't even seem to notice. Dad, having realized what was happening, quickly grabbed him, ripped off his pant leg while simultaneously taking four or five strides to the river and dunking Richie's sizzling leg into the cold water. This happened so fast that the three of us boys, Gramps, and Harry could only look on in stunned amazement. Richie finally realized what was happening and let out a howl like a wild coyote caught in a trap.

Once the danger had passed and Richie calmed down, John, Kunt, and I started laughing and saying, "Liar, liar, pants on fire!" Harry and Gramps also laughed once they realized Richie was OK. "Damn kid is a fireball!" Harry said to Gramps. "He lit up like a cheap cigar!" Gramps exclaimed as John, Kunt, and I joined in the laughter. Dad and Richie came back up from the water, and we toned down our laughter as we watched my crying brother walk back toward us. "See what happens when you turn your back on a fire?!" Dad said to us. All we could do was nod and try not to laugh while Richie pouted and returned to his spot around the fire, this time cautiously facing the flames. Satisfied that a little burned skin would heal up, and after about twenty minutes of rotisserie heating around the fire, Dad ushered us off to our sleeping spot over in the canyon. "Time to hit the sack. You boys have had enough fun for today!"

The sound of birds singing and the way the morning sunlight filtered through the fabric of my dew-covered sleeping bag let me know it was a new day. I'd been here before, and I knew Dad would have the fire going soon with a pot of boiling water for his instant coffee or for some beef or chicken bouillon. The key was to wait for the right moment, before leaving the warmth of your sleeping bag, to saunter over to the campfire. I knew this was the time to fish for morning trout, but it was so warm in the sleeping bag that I didn't want to get out. The other boys were sawing logs, unseen under a pile of sleeping bags, a few feet away. The motivation to finally get up was a "boy boner," caused by my full bladder. I really had to pee! When I couldn't wait another second, I wiggled out of my warm sleeping bag and out into the cold morning air. Steam rose from the rocky ground where my warm pee hit and created a small yellow puddle. Ah, what a relief!

I smelled the campfire smoke and heard the crackling of burning wood and knew Dad was up and building the fire, so I walked over to warm up. Standing by the fire, still not fully awake, I caught a light movement out of the corner of my eye toward the poison oak bushes. Gramps had slept there last night after he and Harry apparently got into a drunken argument, and they'd refused to sleep near each other. He would be hurting for sure once that poison oak started itching his skin. Poor Gramps! I knew how miserable poison oak made me before I learned how to recognize and avoid it. I grabbed the can of worms and headed for my spot, excited by the chance to catch breakfast, after a short detour, that is. Down in the sleeping canyon where I had left the warmth of my sleeping bag just moments before, I gave a light kick into the heap of sleeping bags. "Wake up, dogs, time to catch some fish!" A couple of groans emanated from the pile. Richie, with a burned leg, and Kunt, with a fresh case of poison oak rash, were not yet ready to face the day.

Twin Hills Panthers Forever!

I STARTED MY FINAL SCHOOL year at Twin Hills School in style. I started attending this School in Kindergarten and had known no other schools growing up. Thanks to my apple picking money, I entered the eighth grade wearing a brand-new pair of brown Desert Boots, Levi's brown corduroy jeans, and a nice shirt sporting a colorful pattern of the '70s. We had all made a little money to spend over in Santa Rosa at the Sonoma County Fair in July, during the first part of picking season. We had some laughs, some fights, some new experiences, and a good start at some decent school clothes. All in all, a good summer!

In early September, the long hot summer days were gone, just like the Gravenstein apples, but the Golden Delicious and other late apples were still waiting to be picked from the trees. The Golden Delicious were a sweet and tasty variety for school lunches, and I couldn't get enough of them. I grabbed a few fresh off the trees outside our house before walking up to school, so I could trade them for a candy bar, a Hostess Fruit Pie, or a bag of potato chips—all lunch items not seen in our house.

Heading into my final year at Twin Hills School was bittersweet. Dad used to line my brothers and me up outside for haircuts and shear us like sheep down to the skin. We took turns whimpering as we sat in the chair for the Marine Corps ritual that Dad had endured, on his way to Korea when he was sixteen years old. If we protested or cried, he said, "Shut up or I'll give you something to cry about, and I'll take your ears off too!" There were a few other boys at school who got the same treatment, and we would call each other "Baldy" while pointing and laughing. This year, much to my delight, Dad left my hair alone, and I let it grow long like my friends at school.

The kids I grew up with at Twin Hills will always be near and dear to my heart because even though we had our differences, we all shared a common education and experience. The teachers were all good people who loved kids and loved to teach, and they were in it for the long haul.

My brothers and I couldn't wait to see the list of names posted on the glass doors of the classrooms a couple of weeks before the school year started. We would check every day until at last they appeared overnight!

"I got Mr. Vann this year!" I announced to my brothers.

"I got Mr. Podstata!" Richie said, excitement in his voice.

John announced that his sixth grade teacher would be my favorite, Mr. Pickens. I loved him because he was funny and made learning fun!

Once, while taking a science test in his class, he hocked a loogie into his mouth and said to me, "Dawson, you know what I did with that phlegm? I recycled it." That was his gross sense of humor. He was also our first flag football coach when we started playing other schools in sixth grade and that was the beginning of our three-year, undefeated, dynasty.

I was devastated to learn, during my sophomore year at Analy High School, that Mr. Pickens had died at the young age of thirty-two. He contracted infectious hepatitis while on a trip to Kashmir, India, with his family. Such a tragic loss of a great teacher and coach.

Twin Hills School was my refuge and my home for most of my waking hours. Whether riding bicycles down the slick cement halls, swinging in circles on the end of the long rope attached to the tall flagpole in the front parking lot, walking on the roof, or playing on the grass fields, I and my brothers and the neighborhood kids spent many hours there, even after school and on weekends. As eighth graders, my classmates and I took our rightful ownership as kings of the school.

I loved football and baseball and using my skills developed from tossing apples gave me an incredible accuracy with a football and a baseball for pitching in Little League. Football was my favorite and even though I was a small kid, I could run like the wind.

Sunday afternoons in the fall, watching the Oakland Raiders on our black and white TV with my dad and Gramps, were good times. I fancied myself a right-handed Kenny "The Snake" Stabler, tossing touchdown passes to Fred Biletnikoff and Cliff Branch while coach John Madden cheered from the sidelines. Daryle Lamonica, the "Mad Bomber," was being phased out and Stabler was taking over as quarterback with his shorter but more accurate passing skills.

The Mad Bomber on our flag football team, the Twin Hills Panthers, was a kid named Greg Reeser. Greg had a cannon of a gifted arm and could really let that football fly! I envied him and knew that I would have been our starting quarterback if he wasn't there, because I could run much faster and complete the shorter passes with ease and accuracy. Coach Williams liked Greg's ability to fire a ball way down the field at will, so I was relegated to coming in on offense to run the ball.

Defense was where I was a first stringer, starting in the backfield as one of the two defensive backs, in tandem with my best buddy, Brad Moran. I covered the right side of the field and Brad covered the left.

I played so much during the day at recess, after school, and weekends that I developed an intuitive feel for the game. I also knew every rut, sprinkler head, clump of grass, and rough spot on our home field and used that knowledge to my advantage. Since Brad and I played so much together, it was fun to put the practice into action on game days.

On the upper grass fields at Twin Hills School, we prepared for a third, undefeated season of flag football, led by the clever, loud, and demanding coach Williams. The key to our success was the Williams's playbook and the group of guys playing, who liked each other and had a common goal—well, make that two. Goal one was to win and goal two was to execute our assignment on each play so that we didn't get yelled at by the coach!

As a Quarterback, I was entrusted with Coach Williams's sacred playbook that I kept tucked securely into my back pocket. During a game, I'd take out the playbook at the huddle, open it wide and display it to the other five players, so they could visualize the play and their role. "Power Right, Sweep Right" was also known as play 1. As I showed the X's and O's drawn out on the three-by-five-inch index card of the playbook, I would say clearly and firmly in my best authoritative prepubescent voice, "On 1, ready Breeaaak!"

It was a beautiful experience to watch a simple, well-designed, and well-executed play unfold in front of me after I snapped the ball into my eager hands. The play developed as if in slow motion, Brad out in front looking for a victim of his rough and skilled style of blocking that would upend his opponent and leave them flat on their back, staring up at the sky. David Tabor and Keoki Grey pushed around defenders and herded them off to the right while I patiently ran behind, waiting for the inevitable opening between the running bodies into which I would burst and cut left into open field. If I could cut left, without getting my flag popped out of its socket and sprint out into the open, then it was a foot race to the end zone, which I seldom lost.

The first game of our final season at Twin Hills was on our home turf against the rival Gravenstein Groundhogs, an elementary school from a rural area south of Sebastopol. We knew each other pretty well, both as a team and as a group of guys who would join Analy High School's team the following fall.

In such a small town, we played with and competed against many of the same guys in Little League Baseball during the spring and early summer months. The Gravenstein team had John Fuji at quarterback and Tom Curtis at end, both pretty fast runners.

We conceded the kickoff to the visiting Groundhogs, so they had the ball on offense after our kick pinned them back around their own ten-yard line. Fujii didn't waste any time testing Brad and me in our defensive backfield. He sent Tom Curtis deep and straight over to Brad's side, and once I didn't see anybody running on my side of the field, I sped behind Tom and Brad, intercepting the ball on the first play of the game! I ran it back across the field and along our sideline as the cheerleaders, dressed in purple and gold, cheered me on, leaving the Groundhogs stunned and with only Fuji to beat near the goal line. I ran back left, knowing there was a clump of grass between us, and I skillfully led him right into it as I crossed the goal line for a touchdown. He tripped and nearly fell to the ground. "Fuji, you suck!" I blurted out as I tossed him the ball and rejoined my team to celebrate on the sidelines with coach Williams. Good-natured, competitive fun, I lived for games like this one.

We were smokin' the Hogs pretty good by halftime and the best was yet to come. A friend of mine, Jim Misthos, was a smart and funny guy who did a great imitation of Howard Cosell calling a Monday night NFL game. Jim's mom showed up at every single game to support our team, knowing that her son was usually warming the bench, but she nevertheless cheered us on from the sidelines. I felt both envious and sad for Jim, because even though I was a starter, my parents never came to any games, either at the Twin Hills football field or to watch me pitch Little League games at Ives Park in downtown Sebastopol. That day would be a glorious one for Jim and his mom, and I reveled in their excitement and happiness!

As we were set to begin the second half, coach Williams looked down the sideline of our willing and eager teammates and called out, "Misthos! You're in!" The look on Jim's face was priceless. He turned red as his eyes darted around while he jogged quickly over to get his assignment from the coach.

"Now Jim, I know you practice at End, but Reeser hurt his knee, so I need you to run a sweep to the right at quarterback for us, OK?" Jim stared back at coach in shocked amazement, beet red and pumped up on adrenaline, "OK, coach, 1R sweep right, with me at QB?" He had to repeat it to be sure he wasn't still sitting on the bench and dreaming.

"Just follow your blockers, you're not going to outrun anyone but if you stay behind your blockers, you'll be fine, OK?" coach Williams reiterated. Still in shock and disbelief, Jim took the playbook from my outstretched hand as I advised, "Just open it up flat in your palms to 1R and let the guys see the play and call for the snap on hut one, just like Joe Namath!"

The five starters and Jim took the field for our first play on offense at the beginning of the second half. Williams told the guys to hold their blocks longer than usual to give Big Jim a chance to build up some steam behind them. Looking down the sideline at Mrs. Misthos, you could see the pride and excitement, mixed with nervous worry, written all over her face as her son trotted out with the first team. The guys were all aware of Jim and his mom's loyalty and team spirit, and nobody wanted to be the guy who missed a block to ruin Jim's golden moment.

Jim called out the play in the huddle as he nervously displayed the playbook to five pairs of eager and determined eyes. Keoki told Brad, as they trotted up to the football, "I'll make sure nobody gets him from behind; you lead the way for Jim!" "Ready, break!" yelled Jim, and the team hustled up to the line of scrimmage.

Jim barked out, "Ready . . . , set . . . , hut one!" The football flew into his shaking, sweaty hands. He tucked it under his right arm and ran, wide-eyed and serious, right behind a determined group of blockers! Brad took out Tom Curtis with one of his famous cross-body blocks, upending him and sending his feet skyward and removing his defensive attempt to get to Big Jim, who was rolling like a runaway train, slowly gathering momentum.

There wasn't a defender within ten feet of Jim as he rolled along our sideline in front of a cheering coach Williams, teammates, and Jim's Mom, all shouting, "Go Jim!" Just as he was within ten yards of the goal line, the Groundhog's fastest running defender, Fuji, came flying up behind Jim in hot pursuit. Just as Fuji reached his outstretched arm toward Jim's flag belt, Keoki laid a block on Fuji from the side that knocked him on his back, while Jim scored a glorious touchdown.

The sidelines went wild, high-fiving each other and calling out, "Touchdown Misthos, YES!!" Coach Williams was all smiles and Mrs. Misthos clapped and cried for her son's moment of glory. Keoki reached his big Hawaiian hand down and helped Fuji up from the turf. "You suck, Fuji" he said as they both laughed.

The pride and loyalty of being a Twin Hills Panther, sporting the purple and gold, was something big, special, and important; I felt I was part of a group of kids who were destined to change the world! Coach Williams was a clear and concise taskmaster who instilled in us a sense of confidence and pride. That year, just like the previous two years, we beat all of the other local elementary schools—Brookhaven, Hillcrest, Gravenstein, Oak Grove, Guerneville, and Piner Elementary. Twin Hills ruled!

The Summer of 1976

I TURNED SIXTEEN IN JANUARY of 1976 and the first thing I did in the morning was pop out of bed and say, "Let's go to the DMV in Santa Rosa, Mom. Today, I finally get my driver's license!" I took the driver's test in Mom's 1967 Plymouth Barracuda, a car I had been driving on the backroads since she bought it two years earlier. The traffic on Santa Rosa Avenue was light, and the test was a breeze, so I had my license and could now drive my 1965 GTO. The country's bicentennial celebrations were starting off on a positive note.!

FLEA MARKET FUN

I started working for Russ, a twenty-eight-year-old hippie, who was a hardworking fruit seller, picker, and negotiator, at the flea market south of Sebastopol. Russ had a brilliant business model, and one you probably couldn't learn in business school. He used a combination of cheap child labor, low cost of goods, and all cash transactions to amass enough cash within a few years to buy a hundred acres on top of Mill Creek Road, up in Healdsburg. I was able to drive the trucks that Russ brought the fruit home in,from the Central Valley and the Imperial Valley of Southern California.

I had experimented with alcohol and found the loss of physical control and the lasting hangover dreadful. I preferred the altered state that was brought on after smoking pot, which was dreamlike and mellow. When smoking with a few friends, the uncontrollable laughter that arose was the deep kind of belly laughter that hurt your stomach after laughing so much. I liked the way music became personal and vibrant, along with the added euphoria that anything seemed possible.

Russ and I smoked pot out of an old tobacco pipe as we drove down to the fruit-filled Central Valley in California on those warm summer evenings of 1976. The 1965 Dodge one-ton box truck was loaded with empty wooden lug boxes that we filled in the mornings with oranges, grapefruit, or apricots, that the two of us picked fresh from the trees.

Russ would typically strike up a conversation with an old farmer and most of the time he was told the entire crop had been purchased by Safeway, or one of the other big chain grocery stores. That was perfect, Russ would reason with the farmer, because surely those big boys wouldn't miss a few boxes, and besides, we would pick, box, and load the fruit ourselves.

The old farmer would hem and haw awhile before saying, "Yeah, go ahead and fill your boxes then. Give me ten dollars for my trouble and I guess that'll be OK. That big chain store buyer beat me down on price anyway."

Once the deal was sealed, we unloaded the empty wooden lug boxes out of the truck in a discreet location on the old boy's ranch and got to work in the hot, dusty orange grove. I was a skinny kid and those boxes full of fruit weighed about a third of what I did, so I worked up a sweat in no time and slept like a dog at night.

My diet during that year of my young life was almost exclusively fruit. I ate whatever was in season, so I was never hungry. One of my favorites was watermelon. Driving up through the hot summer valley without air conditioning in the old truck required that I occasionally pull the truck off to the side of the road for some refreshment. I would walk around to the back of the truck and grab a big ripe watermelon, drop it on the hot pavement, and pick up the heart of the melon to eat, while leaving the rest. Cool, sweet, red, ripe watermelon on a hot summer day, nothing better!

Midgley's Country Flea Market on Gravenstein Highway South, just past Bloomfield Road, was where the fun and the cash flowed on warm summer weekends. Long rows of makeshift tables locked end to end filled the large upward sloped and otherwise barren grounds of the market. The tables were nothing more than four-by-eight-foot sheets of cheap plywood, supported by sawhorses. The thin, wooden overhead structures that encompassed two rows of tables and the aisle between them, which supported blue tarps over some of the tables, plastic corrugated roofing in other places, and several tables that remained unprotected from the summer sun.

The tables at the top of the hill and around the outer perimeter where unshaded and usually served as overflow for first timers rather than the more premium spots claimed by regular vendors. Russ paid a premium for the first spot on the right as shoppers entered the market from the parking lot.

Early in the morning when the air still carried a foggy chill, we had backed the truck into position and unloaded boxes full of the day's offerings. Oranges fresh from the trees of Porterville; lemons; grapefruits; local Gravenstein apples; dates from Indio; and watermelons from El Centro. All set up for the day, I ventured through the market where only a few early birds were watching vendors unload their wares, hoping to be the first one to spot a treasure and a bargain.

This time, in the early stillness of the day, watching the market come to life was my time to explore and learn. What is it? How does it work? How old is it? Where did you find it? If I was interested at all in a particular item, the last question was always how much?

That question kicked off the fun part of any flea market transaction!

Someone had told me that if you ever visit the markets in Mexico you barter for everything, and it was the same at the flea market. If you didn't barter, it was considered an insult. Anyone who asks a price and then hands over the amount right away is considered a fool.

A shrewd merchant will watch you closely without you even being aware. When you see something that really piques your interest, the merchant is very sensitive to your "tell," as it is referred to by poker players. That slight gleam in your eyes, that thin smile on your face, the raising of an eyebrow. Once the merchant sees it, he will cast out his bait by saying, "That is a rare and beautiful item right there," or some such lure. Let the bargaining game begin!

As I wandered through the early morning market, I spotted an eight-track tape player that I thought would be perfect for my 1965 Pontiac GTO. I acted indifferent as I picked it up from the table to inspect the condition and features. It was exactly what I wanted. So I put it back on the table and looked at a few other items before finally asking the man behind the table, "What do you want for the old tape player there?" He replied, "Oh, I don't know, how about ten dollars?"

I acted uninterested by letting out a small "hmmmm," as I continued grabbing and examining a few other items. I picked up a set of end wrenches and asked, "How about these?" To which he replied, "Twelve dollars." I let out another "hmmmm" and continued down along his table to look through a box of eight-track tapes that had fifty cents written on each one.

I looked up at the man and asked, "How many of these tapes are you gonna throw in with that old five dollar tape player?" He countered, "The tapes are fifty cents each and the tape player I can let go for seven dollars." "Well," I said, "if you give me the player for five, then I'll have two dollars left to buy six of these tapes!"

"I don't know what kinda math they taught you in school, boy, but I tell you what, you can have the tape player and four tapes for seven." To which I agreed and picked out tapes of the Steve Miller Band, Elvin Bishop, Led Zeppelin, and Lou Reed after handing over the seven dollars. "Thanks, man," I said as I took my prize back in the direction of our fruit stand. "You stole it from me," the merchant said jokingly with a smile.

I continued up the aisle looking for anything interesting— car-related parts and tools, shifters, chrome, Stewart-Warner gauges, sun tachometers, car magazines, or repair manuals. The hard nipples of braless hippy chicks caught my adolescent eye and put a shy smile across my face as I sauntered around the market.

As the crowds started coming in, I headed back to the fruit stand to get to work. "Check it out man!" I said to Russ as he was bagging a dollar's worth of oranges for a customer. "That's ten pounds of sweet and juicy fruit right there," he said to the man, pointing to the dial indicator on the scale. "Have a nice day."

Russ looked over at the tapes and tape deck and asked, "How much?" To which I replied, "Seven bucks and he threw in the four tapes." Russ smiled and said, "Well, that's about a day's pay for you, so you better get busy bagging those oranges for this fine young lady." He nodded to a hippy chick who was savoring a sample slice of orange. She smiled at Russ's compliment as he eyed her up and down.

The carnival-like atmosphere of the market became livelier as the sun grew warmer and more crowds filtered through the gates. The old farmers, Mexicans, hippies, and young and old, were all looking for something.

On most summer weekends, my buddy Steve would walk down to the market from his house up near Bloomfield Road, and if it wasn't too busy, we would smoke a joint and bullshit. He wandered through the market stoned and smiling, while I, in a similar state, resumed bagging fruit.

Russ had built up a pretty good number of regular customers, some of whom came to the market solely for the fresh fruit on our tables. It seemed the fruit offerings changed with each weekend, sometimes oranges, sometimes watermelons, cantaloupes, or dates and dried banana chips.

One regular, an old gentleman who dressed in a dark suit and tie, complete with a black derby hat and suspenders, came every weekend and went through the same routine. He would instruct me, in a slow and deliberate manner, to put various items in a bag. I totaled the cost of the items in my head and told him the price. If the total came to one dollar and fifty cents, for example, he would retrieve an old leather coin purse from his pocket and very slowly open it up to finger the coins deliberately before handing me two quarters. I looked at him and said very respectfully, "The total for your fruit is one dollar and fifty cents, sir." He would nod and say, "Thank you, young man" and carry away his fruit-filled bag. Russ and I would just look at each other and laugh while he playfully said to me, "You let that old man con you. That's coming out of your pay!"

This routine with the old man went on week after week, until one Saturday he had me fill up a bag of shiny apples while he carefully watched. I told him that it was a dollar's worth of apples and, as usual, he fished two quarters out of his old leather coin purse and handed them to me.

On this particular day, he asked to leave his bag at our table so he could browse the rest of the market. He'd be back to pick them up on his way out the gate. As he disappeared into the crowd, I grabbed his bag of apples and dumped them back into the box from which I'd taken them. I grabbed the box of over-ripe and rotten apples from the back of the truck and refilled his bag with partially fermenting apples, then set it back on the table with the top folded over.

The man came by and grabbed the bag on his way out. I hoped he would wait until he got home to look inside, which was exactly what happened. I snickered as I said to Russ, "That will teach him to screw us!"

The following Saturday in came the old man, sauntering by in his suit as usual. He stopped in front of our table, directly across from me, and as he pointed his finger he said, "You, young man, you put the 'fertilizer' in my apples!" That was about the funniest thing I had ever heard—referring to rotten apples as fertilizer. I burst out laughing as he stared at me with a flat expression. I continued laughing until Russ acted appalled and offered the man a new bag of apples. I denied knowing anything about the "fertilizer" in his apples, but he knew better. He never left a bag at our table again, but he also continued to pay only two quarters and to remind me every weekend, "You, young man, you put the fertilizer in my apples!"

Occasionally, during a fast and furious day, I stuffed a twenty dollar bill into my sock as my self-ordained bonus for all of my hard work and knowing the low cost of the fruit that I sweated to pick, load, unload, and bag up for the customers. Russ knew and never said anything; I assumed he figured it was only fair, especially since at the end of the day he counted himself a nice stack of tax-free cash.

In retrospect, that old man and I weren't very different. He paid what the fruit was worth to him, and I paid myself what I thought my labor was worth.

The following week in July, an event occurred along Highway 99 near the town of Chowchilla that I'll never forget.

I was cruising north with all of the windows rolled down, headed back home in Russ's 1972 Dodge van, with a sweaty load of cantaloupes. In the mid-July, 100-plus degree heat, those melons sweated so badly that the smell was almost unbearable! I drank lots of water, but the heat still made me a little drowsy, especially after picking all of those cantaloupes in the early morning down in Bakersfield.

As I drove along, I glanced back at the sweaty melons, loaded into the van's cargo area without the benefit of crates and noticed that the double side doors were starting to bulge outward. I kept a wary eye on them to see if the weight of the melons would push the doors further outward, and I imagined the mess on the highway behind me if they suddenly burst open.

Distracted by the pending potential disaster, I hardly noticed the two police cars who came up fast behind me. I assumed they would fly past toward whatever big bust they were after, but their flashing lights stayed directly behind me.

I gently pulled off to the right side of the road, wondering what minor traffic infraction I might have committed. Did I accidentally swerve when I turned to check the melon situation behind my seat? I knew I wasn't speeding.

Once I came to a complete stop, I sat nervously in the van wondering what was going on, because the two police officers had excited their patrol cars and cautiously approached my van with guns drawn.

I was already sweating like one of the melons, but now I felt sick as well. The cop who came to my side ordered me, at gunpoint, to put both hands on the steering wheel. I did as I was instructed and slowly glanced through the passenger side window down the barrel of another police weapon. I was told to exit the vehicle as he opened the door for me and to go around to the other side, very slowly, and open the side doors. Rather than argue, I did as I was told after gently saying the van was full of cantaloupes that would spill out if I opened the doors. The three of us watched as the melons spilled out onto the hot pavement and revealed nothing that they were looking for in their quest to fight crime.

The weapons were holstered, and apologies were made as I prepared to pick up the melons. Apparently, there had been a kidnapping of some schoolkids, and the perpetrators used a white Dodge van as part of their scheme. "Sorry, have a good day, sir," the officer said as he and his partner walked back to their cars and took off. I picked up most of the hot melons and was thankful I didn't get shot. I got home late that night but made sure to read the newspaper the next morning:

1976 Bus Kidnapping

On July 15, 1976, a busload of children aged five to fourteen, and their school bus driver, Ed Ray (age 55), were abducted on a country road in Madera County at about 4 p.m., on their way back from a swim outing at the fairgrounds. The bus was later found empty and covered with bamboo and brush in a drainage ditch nine miles west of town. The victims, nineteen girls and seven boys, along with Ray, were driven around for eleven hours in two vans before being entombed in a moving van buried in a Livermore rock quarry.

After sixteen hours underground in an 8 foot by 16-foot space, the victims dug their way out and were found in a remote area near the Shadow Cliffs East Bay Regional Park. They were then taken to the nearby Santa Rita Rehabilitation Center, where they were pronounced in good condition. The children and their bus driver returned safely to Chowchilla by a police-escorted bus shortly before dawn on July 17, 1976.

Investigators dug up the van and learned it had been buried in the quarry in November 1975. The 100-acre Portola Valley estate of the quarry owner, Frederick Nickerson Woods, was searched. Woods' son, Fred Newhall Woods IV, 24, was missing.

Authorities issued an all-points bulletin for young Woods and his two friends, James Schoenfeld, 24, and his brother, Richard Schoenfeld, 22, sons of a wealthy podiatrist. Officials said they discovered a rough draft of a $5 million ransom note on the Woods estate. Source: City of Chowchilla Website

TIJUANA

Two weeks later, Russ and I would venture all the way down to San Diego for a self-pick load of avocados and my first visit over the border to Tijuana, Mexico.

Russ parked his 1965 Dodge one-ton box truck in a huge parking lot on the US side, and we walked across the border into Mexico. We hailed a taxi, a dented rattle-trap Ford LTD, and before we could give the driver our destination he asked us, in a thick Mexican accent, "You boys looking for pussy?"

I was a sixteen-year-old virgin, but I wasn't looking to get laid in a whorehouse in Mexico. I was more interested in bartering for a few switchblade knives that I could take home and sell to my buddies. I had also heard that they let sixteen-year-olds into bars, so maybe a cold beer was on the agenda. The cab driver dropped us off downtown in the thick of things after asking, "What you looking for boys? Pussy?" a few more times.

I immediately fell in love with the market streets of Tijuana and was amazed at what sat on the tables and in display cases for sale. Pistols, fireworks, and all types of knives, including the switchblade type that I was looking for. There were Mexican sombrero hats for the tourists, along with pinatas and colorful clay figures.

Russ went into a bar while I stayed outside on the busy sidewalk, taking in the tremendous variety of market goods. It didn't take long before I started to barter in Spanish for the first of the four knives I would eventually buy. "Cuánto por ese cuchillo, señor?" (How much for that knife, mister?). The vendor looked at me, a young "gringo" with long hair and a worn-out, brown leather jacket and started off the bartering with his reply, "Para ti, mi amigo, solo diez dólares Americanos!" (For you my friend, only ten American dollars!). I gave him a sour look and countered with, "Oh no, señor, eso es demasiado muy caro. Me gusta solo por cinco dólares y no mas!" (Oh no, sir, that's very expensive. I like it for five dollars and no more!). The vendor shot back a hurt expression, as if I had just called his mother a whore and loudly pronounced back his "best final offer," which in reality is rarely best or final. "Este cuchillo es major que todos los demás en este mercado, pero para ti, amigo, lo vender por seven dollars." (This knife is better than all the others at this market, but for you, my friend, I will sell it for seven dollars.). I feigned disinterest and replied with *my* best and final offer, "Seis dólares o nada señor, hay muchos cuchillos en el mercado y otros mejores y más baratos también!" (Six dollars or nothing sir, there are many more knives in the marketplace and others better and cheaper too!). I slowly started to walk away to the next table as the vendor said, "OK amigo, solo una vez, seis dólares por este cuchillo." (OK buddy, one time only, six dollars for this knife). I handed him the cash and put the switchblade in the pocket of my jacket while I eyed the other goods on the next display table.

I repeated this bartering process three more times until I felt satisfied that I had gotten the best four switchblades at the lowest possible price.

I dragged Russ out of the dark and loud cantina, where a topless lady was whipping the men into a frenzy with her naked gyrations. A group of four men greeted patrons on their way out the door, including Russ and I, with the now familiar Tijuana greeting, "Looking for pussy, boys?"

Russ staggered out and into the semi-lit street as his eyes adjusted. "Let's get out of here if you're done getting whatever you wanted to get," he said to me.

"I got four sweet switchblades, but it sure took a lot of bartering. I'm ready to go," I replied. "Vámonos, cabron!"

We got into the back of a different beat-up taxi and headed back to the pedestrian border crossing. We would walk back to the truck and head north. One last time, we heard the "Tijuana anthem" from the cabbie, "Pussy, boys? You looking for pussy?" to which Russ and I laughed at the same time and replied, "No gracias amigo, vamos a Estados Unidos, ahora!"

Side by side we stood in a line of "returnees" to San Diego, Russ with his dirty whitewashed-straw cowboy hat, long beard, and blond ponytail and me, a sixteen-year-old long-haired kid who looked twelve years old. Four shiny, new switch blades sat in the front pockets of my brown leather jacket, two knives per pocket.

As we approached the Border Patrol agents at the entry point, both of us had our driver's licenses in hand for what we assumed would be a quick wave of the agent's hand to proceed back across the border. It turned out that leaving Mexico was a lot harder than coming into Mexico!

After showing my driver's license, brand new only eight months prior, the agent asked if I was bringing anything home with me? Hoping for a smooth walk through, like so many ahead of us in line had experienced, I simply replied, "No, sir." I've always been a terrible liar and the agent must have sniffed out my lie like a hound dog on a coon's scent, because he immediately pulled me out of line for a pat down. The four switchblades in my pockets were quickly confiscated, and the agent asked if I had anything else that I didn't think to mention. "No, sir," I replied as he led me to an isolation room while Russ was led to a different room for further inquiry.

They asked who Russ was and how long I'd known him, to which I truthfully replied that he was my boss and that I'd known him a couple of years. I explained that we picked fruit in California and that I had never been to Tijuana, so Russ brought me for a few hours. I apologized for lying about the knives and told them that I'd spent almost all of my time here bargaining for them.

The agent asked if I had my parent's permission to be out of the country, since I was only sixteen years old. I lied and said, "Sure, my mom knows where I am!" Well, they called Mom at home; I didn't know if she'd be there or at work. She answered the phone and when asked if she knew her son was at the Mexican border with a man named Russ, she replied, "Yes, I knew they were going down that way." In fact, Mom had no idea where I was most of the time, but her monotone consent was good enough for the agents.

They handed me a citation for international smuggling and Russ paid the $40.00 fine right then and there. The knives that I had so patiently bargained for were gone. They let us both go, and we walked back toward the fruit truck in the parking lot.

We both exchanged our stories of being separated and questioned. Russ always carried a stack of cash, just in case he came across a good deal for fruit that he could resell at a profit. The agents questioned him about the cash, to which he responded,

"I was looking to score some weed, but it didn't work out." The agents reluctantly let Russ keep his cash.

As we approached a drinking fountain, Russ stuck his finger down his throat and threw up a small plastic baggie with a few joints worth of weed in it and a tiny paper bindle that contained a half-gram of cocaine. He told me he had both things stashed in his cheek while we stood in line and when they separated us into the two different rooms for questioning, he swallowed everything.

When we got back to the truck, Russ turned on the defroster so he could dry out the newspaper bindle of coke. I had never seen cocaine before, let alone snort it, but as soon as it was dry, Russ cut it up with his small pocket knife. We each snorted some right then and there before heading home. I didn't feel much of anything, but that may have been the sense of excitement and relief I felt after my first Tijuana experience.

Back home, Mom never mentioned anything about the trip or the call from the Border Patrol. I think she was more anxious about the impending and inevitable move to join Dad, Gramps, and my brothers up in Lakeport. The Longs Drug Store construction and stocking was finished so Mom and I prepared to make the 70 mile move North to Lakeport. I begged her to stay here, in Sebastopol, but she reminded me that I needed to get up there to start my junior year at Clearlake High School, the day after Labor Day weekend. Sadly, the summer of 1976 was over.

The Carefree Days
of High School

FEB 1977

First thing in the morning, as I was getting ready to leave for school at Clearlake High School, my hungover dad handed me a twenty-five dollar check, drawn on Mom's account. As he handed me the check, he said, "You want to make your own rules and not follow mine, then hit the road and don't come back!" I just took the check with my right hand, still in a white plaster cast up to my elbow, without saying a word.

I wanted to ask him, "What the hell happened to you? Why did you move the family up here to live in this shithole? Why don't you man up and get a job like a responsible father and husband? Don't you have any pride at all?"

I wanted to ask him what ever became of the loving, caring, smart, and funny man that could do anything? I wondered how he couldn't see how far down his drinking had taken him—and the rest of the family. I wondered if he even gave a shit.

I knew that what I said wouldn't make any difference to him. He was a raging lunatic who was enabled by a terrified wife and two younger boys steeped in denial of his wrongdoing and trying to survive.

I knew it was a bad omen when the air came out of the rear air shocks of my 1965 Pontiac GTO during my move up here to Lakeport from my home in Sebastopol, only five short months ago.

The previous afternoon I had pushed my drunken Dad to the floor in a final act of defiance. I was standing in the living room/kitchen of the small duplex unit that the family was crammed into, talking to my brothers, Rich and John, when Dad walked in wavering and mumbling to himself.

We all greeted him warily. I stood blowing bubblegum bubbles with a popping sound several yards away from him. "Don't blow bubbles in my face!" he sneered at me from across the room. I replied, "What are you talking about? I'm nowhere near you," as I continued chewing and blowing bubbles. He stumbled across the room and landed a glancing blow on the side of my face as he repeated, "Don't blow bubbles in my face goddammit!" I stood there silently and defiantly staring back at him, wanting to strike back but knowing there would be consequences. I blew another bubble and popped it as he started to walk away. He swung around and hit me in the face with a clenched fist once again. This time, I decided I wasn't going to take his shit anymore. I avoided the urge to punch him back hard and I instead pushed him backward with both hands, knocking him off balance and sending him sprawling on the floor. As he fell to the floor, my two younger brothers just stood there stunned. I ran outside through the front door, jumped into my 1956 GMC pickup, and drove away.

I drove my old pickup truck out into a walnut orchard and listened to Lou Reed's *Rock 'n' Roll Animal* and the Steve Miller Band's *Book of Dreams* on my eight-track tape player. I thought about what might happen next.

Once enough time had passed, I reasoned that Dad would be passed out and asleep back at the duplex. I drove the pickup slowly up the gravel road and parked. I slipped in through the back door and into my bed, in the room shared with my brothers, for the last time.

The next morning, after silently taking the twenty-five-dollar check from Dad's hand, I loaded up a small wooden chest of drawers that contained all of my worldly possessions and placed it into the bed of my old pickup truck. The ratty old chest of drawers contained three pairs of jeans, a half-dozen pairs of socks, a few pairs of underwear, about a dozen T-shirts, a brass pipe elbow fitting that I smoked pot in, and a few books I planned to read at some point.

Hard to believe that only five months prior, back in Sebastopol, I had loaded up the same old, ratty chest of drawers into the car I'd bought the year before, a Canary Yellow 1965 Pontiac GTO, with $250.00 of my apple-picking money.

April 1975

Just a year and a half prior, in the spring of 1975, I was fifteen years old when I bought the GTO from my childhood friend Dale. Dale's Dad had bought him a nice 1969 Buick GS Skylark for his sixteenth birthday, so Dale didn't mind parting with his 965 GTO. Until I got my driver's license in January of 1976,

I drove it on the back roads of west Sebastopol, up Burnside Road or to Pleasant Hill Road, down Bloomfield Road, and then back down Burnside to home. I cleaned out the old garage/small barn that had been used over the years as a horse barn for my sister, Debbie and as a chicken coop for the free-range chickens that only needed a safe place to roost at night. The floor was literally covered with a thick layer of an obnoxious combination of layered horse hay, horseshit, and chickenshit.

The center truss beam functioned as the chickens' roost, which the chickens accessed one step at a time up a twelve-foot, wooden apple-picking ladder. They would squawk and jockey for position all along the wooden beam, until they were evenly spaced from wall to wall across the top of the barn. The evening droppings created a pyramid of chicken shit all along the center of the floor, which was the entire width of the garage under the beam.

I used a large flat shovel, known to me as a "horseshit" shovel, normally used to clean horse stalls, to clean out a place for my GTO so I could work on it there until I could, the following year, drive it to school and cruise 4th Street in Santa Rosa on Saturday nights. It took three long hard days of shoveling to reveal an ancient concrete floor. I did what my slim budget would allow and installed a used eight-track tape player, purchased at Midgley's Country Flea Market for five dollars under the dash of the GTO. I had only two tapes, Elvis Bishop's *Juke Joint Jump* and *Led Zeppelin II*, and I wore them out while working on the car in the newly cleaned shop.

As I made money picking fruit and working at the flea market, I added parts to the GTO: a chrome, barefoot gas pedal and Gabriel Hijackers air shocks that came in a box with a picture of a cartoon rabbit. I liked the dragster look—big wide tires in back, rear jacked up like a stink bug, and low in front with skinny stock tires. I added new, shiny chrome rims on back with wide Grand Auto tires, but the front still had stock black rims without hubcaps.

The hood had flown off on the freeway before I owned it, so I drove it without a hood to show off all the chrome on the 389 V8 motor. I added JC Whitney's finest automobile black carpet, along with STP and Hurst Shifter stickers on the driver's side rear window. I was cool!

September 1976

I made the long, gloomy sixty-five-mile trek over the winding Hopland Grade, a.k.a. Route 175, to Lakeport. I had waited until the very last day to leave home in Sebastopol before rejoining the rest of the family and starting my junior year of high school, at Clearlake High in Lakeport.

As an omen of things to come, the rear air shocks started to lose air going over the steep and curvy grade, causing the body to drop onto the wide rear tires and dig into the sidewalls. I heard the inner fenders scraping the tires as smoke billowed out behind me, so I pulled off the road to assess the damage. The plastic line to the air shocks had contacted the hot exhaust pipe, creating a leak and loss of air to the shocks. I left my broken-down car and hitchhiked the remaining ten miles to the family's duplex on Tortilla Flats, the derogatory name for Linda Lane. I returned about an hour later with electrical tape and a bicycle pump, which I used to fix the melted airline and pump air back into the shocks. Down the hill I drove to my new home in Lakeport.

I started high school in Lakeport and wanted to play football on the JV team as a junior, because I was still small at five foot six and 130 pounds, but the coach said I had to play on the varsity team with the big boys or nothing, so I hooked up instead with the stoners and the auto shop guys.

Still shy and afraid of girls, I fit in where I could to survive. The auto shop was a lot better than the old, dark barn of a shop back at Analy High School in Sebastopol, and I liked it a lot. I was as smart or smarter than all the other kids there, just like I had always been growing up, but I dumbed down, kept quiet, tried to fit in, and stayed under the radar.

I rebuilt the motor in my history teacher's car in exchange for an A and never had to go to his class. I learned how to weld and took lots of welding classes during the day and at night. The only way to get better at welding is to practice a lot, so my friends and I would smoke a fat joint before class and weld for hours.

The clutch in my GTO started to fail from too many burnouts, so I traded it for a neighbor's 1956 GMC pickup truck and a non-running 1965 Honda 305 Dream motorcycle. I had always liked the style of old trucks, and this one had the original six-cylinder engine coupled to a "3 on the tree" transmission. I had the idea that I could load up the motorcycle in the bed of the truck and cruise it around Sebastopol when I visited on weekends.

I managed to get the Honda running. It was a heavy motorcycle and not so nimble, but that did not keep me from riding around the cow pastures surrounding Tortilla Flats with our landlord, an old hippy named Dick, who rode his Triumph Bonneville 650 in the fields with me. Dick was an agricultural pump repairman by day. A nice man, he rented a room to my Grandpa in the duplex next to the one my family occupied.

Much as it had been in Sebastopol, Gramps was a calming presence during my dad's loud, obnoxious storms. He smoked pot to help himself breathe and sleep better, with his one lung still keeping him going. "Danny, this whole marijuana being illegal is a big sham. It will be legal again in a few years, you'll see," Gramps said as he passed the joint to me. I took a small toke, passed the joint to Dick, and replied, "I sure think you are right, Gramps. People who drink alcohol sure do get mean and crazy, but everyone I know who smokes pot just wants to laugh and have fun in a peaceful, mellow way."

Dad drank himself out of his latest radio station job in Lakeport fairly soon after Mom and I arrived from Sebastopol, and since Mom needed their only car to drive to Longs Drugs store in Ukiah where she worked, he decided he could just take my truck to go back and forth to the Buckhorn Saloon and drink all day. That left me to bum rides to school or to ride the Honda. Luckily, my hotrod car friends were great and would pick me up and get me home.

Gary B. would usually pick me up in the morning, so we could get stoned on our way to school in his 1965 Mustang that he'd bought for twenty-five dollars. He was a funny guy and flirted with all the girls. Gary and his brother, Glenn, were my welding class buddies. I felt like I was starting to fit in and meet more people, but then four days before Thanksgiving in 1976, the Honda 305 Dream became my worst nightmare!

November 1976

I rode the Honda down to the south end of Lakeport to pick up a newspaper at dusk, and on my way back home a 1962 Nova turned left into a propane gas office. I hit the center of its bumper going about thirty-five miles per hour. I do not remember anything after that. I woke up four days later, on Thanksgiving Day, in the Ukiah Hospital, with my right arm in a blood-soaked cast in traction, a cast on my left forearm, and another cast on my right ankle. The guy who hit me told me later in the hospital that I cartwheeled over his car. My arm took out a row of mailboxes on a wooden platform, my helmet popped off my head, and I ended up in a ditch, with blood pouring out of my ears and nose and both bones of my right arm sticking out of the bloody skin. He thought for sure that he had killed me.

The pain in my right forearm was unbearable and swelled up so tight inside the cast that the doctors removed and replaced the cast six times. They literally screwed a stainless-steel plate, about one inch wide by four inches long, onto my right arm bone to hold it together, along with a stainless steel pin through my wrist. Every time I woke up, I screamed in pain, and after a shot of morphine I was back asleep.

There were no visits from my family, apparently they all had more important things to do. I did have a short one from Dad and the guy who collided with me, who was very concerned and apologetic. He brought me what he thought would cheer up any sixteen-year-old boy: a fresh copy of *Playboy* magazine. I knew the guy was trying to be helpful, but it was only a source of frustration for me, as drooling over the hot centerfold model left me with a boner and no way to touch it with both hands wrapped in casts.

Out of necessity, I learned to eat left-handed, and as brutal as it was knowing how beat-up my body was, I felt better being in the hospital than in the shithole duplex up on Tortilla Flats. The first thing I asked the doctor, other than "What the hell happened?" was if I would still be able to pitch a baseball or throw a football, to which he sadly shook his head and said, "You are lucky to still have your arm and luckier still to be alive!"

I would have a cast on my arm for the next three months and then after a year, they would slice down the middle of the horrendous scar on my right forearm and remove the steel plate screwed to my bone. Any athletic aspirations had come to an abrupt halt. As I lay in the hospital, I remember thinking that all I ever wanted was a normal family, whatever "normal" meant. A supportive place to navigate the difficulties of being a teenager trying to figure out life. Why did we have to leave our home in Sebastopol?

Laying in the hospital gave me plenty of time to reflect on the previous two years since leaving Twin Hills and starting high school without my best friend, Brad, who had been like a big brother to me since fifth grade. He had moved with his family to Sonoma before the start of high school, and I'd felt alone in a bigger world ever since.

Brad and I had played flag football, baseball, basketball, and Junior Olympics together, hung out at school and a lot after school at his house up by the old Spring Hill School and abandoned cemetery in a Eucalyptus grove. I worked sometimes for Brad's dad in early summer, before the Gravenstein apples were ready to pick, bagging ice and loading bags and blocks on the conveyor belt in his ice vending trailer at the Shell gas station in south Sebastopol, across the street from Furusho Brothers apple packing company When high school started without my best friend, it was a strange and frightening world.

I got straight A's and played freshman football as the smallest kid on the team at five foot four and ninety-eight pounds. I made the varsity tennis team as a freshman after just learning the game the previous summer, and I felt good about that even though I felt like I should have been pitching on the baseball team after being a Little League pitcher for five years. I wanted to explore other sports and experiences and, honestly, I didn't think I was good enough to pitch in high school.

I was starting to settle into this big high school world where Dad had landed a part-time job teaching ROTC electronics. My friends thought he was funny, but he was an embarrassment to me, especially when my English teacher told me, in front of everyone in class, about a short exchange she had with my dad in the school quad area.

Dad was walking toward the shop classroom, where the electronics class would start in about thirty minutes, smoking a Camel and crossing the quad as students lounged in the sun during lunchtime. Mrs. Forte spotted him and said, "Excuse me, sir, but you can't smoke on this campus!" Introductions were made as Dad snuffed out his cigarette on the pavement, and they both laughed about it. After a year, he quit his job at Analy High School and took a position as chief engineer at a new radio station in Lakeport.

Mom was in line to become the first woman to manage a Longs Drugs store, but the store she slated to manage was still under construction and located up north in Ukiah. Dad got a job at the radio station in Lakeport and took my brothers and

Grandpa up there with him. Mom and I stayed in Sebastopol for the next year.

The time that Mom and I lived in Sebastopol, in a drama-free household, was wonderful. Dad wasn't around to bust my balls, and my brothers weren't around to steal my stuff and harass me. I was becoming more independent and mature, figuring out life. Sister Deb was living in Santa Rosa, and she came around occasionally now that Dad was gone. Mom and I went to her high school graduation ceremony at Santa Rosa High School in June of 1976.

I turned sixteen in January of 1976, and the first thing in the morning I popped out of bed and said, "Let's go to the DMV in Santa Rosa, Mom. Today I finally get my driver's license!"

I took the driving test in Mom's 1967 Plymouth Barracuda, a car I had been driving on the backroads since she'd bought it two years earlier. The traffic on Santa Rosa Avenue was light that day and the test was a breeze, so I had my license and now I could drive my 1965 GTO. The bicentennial celebrations of the US were starting off on a positive note !

Back to February 1977

Fortunately, I could shift the column three speed on my pickup truck and drive, even with the cast on my right forearm. It was early February and driving over the Hopland Grade, you had to be careful not to hit an icy corner. Although it had been a dry winter thus far, you had to be careful on the mountain because there were corners that never saw the sun in winter.

I was happy to finally go back home to Sebastopol. I had the old faithful pickup truck and the twenty-five dollars, along with a huge sense of relief, that no matter what happened, I was no longer stuck with my asshole-alcoholic Dad, who didn't care about anyone but himself!

Halfway to Sebastopol, not exactly sure where I was going in Sebastopol, I stopped in the tiny town of Cloverdale to visit my sister, Deborah, who shared a party house apartment in the middle of town with her boyfriend.

Dave was an OK dude. He let me cruise his 1969 Plymouth Roadrunner around town so he could get rid of me and have his way with my sister. The big car had some get up and go with a 383 V8 and a four speed. I had fun driving it around. I stayed on the couch in my sister's apartment and walked down to the Cloverdale Citrus Fair to look around and check out the cute girls.

I drank beer and smoked pot and listened to Lynyrd Skynyrd and other rock and roll staples like Led Zeppelin, Ronnie Montrose, Pink Floyd, Jeff Beck, and Robin Trower. The fun really started when all the Harley dudes from Santa Rosa showed up with a big sack of "goodies!"

Being Deborah's brother, I was considered cool with the older crowd. One night, I ended up getting all jacked up on speed and walked the streets with a girl who said the chief of police was her dad. We stole houseplants off people's porches while they slept. Why? Seemed like an OK idea at the time; I was just hanging out with the crazy girl.

One of the biker dudes sat in my sister's living room telling me about his recovery from drug addiction, and he was sincere about warning me not to fuck up my life. I was attentive but did not see a problem with the way I was living. I just knew I was too smart to get hooked on anything. My short-lived stay at my sister's place was a nonstop party, and a few days was enough for me, so off I went toward Sebastopol, where I hoped I would be welcomed at Russ and Linda's place.

When I arrived in Sebastopol, I slept in my pickup truck for a few nights out in the apple orchards on Blackney and Pleasant Hill roads. Apparently, Russ had let his dick do his thinking for him when he was caught boning a young lady who worked with him on the weekends at the flea market. Linda found out, and they were in a terrible fight just as I knocked on their door, looking for a place to stay.

Within minutes of being told by Russ that there was no chance of me staying with them, my old buddy Dale showed up to see how I was doing. Dale said, "No problem, just come out to our house. We have plenty of room." Seemed like a good idea at the time and I was getting tired of sleeping in my truck, so I welcomed the invitation.

I dream of being the Windshield, but I'm feeling like a Bug!

ONCE I SETTLED BACK INTO Sebastopol, at the Newman's country farm out on Furlong Road, I let Dale talk me into trading my 1956 Chevy truck for a VW dune buggy owned by my former best friend from Twin Hills School, Brad. I had ridden in it a couple of years earlier when Brad tore through our old apple orchard and we went airborne over the lower terraces of the orchard. As I set off in the truck with Dale to consummate the trade, I dreamed of bikini-clad girls at Salmon Creek Beach, while music of The Beach Boys rang in my head. Endless summer, here we come!

The dune buggy had a faulty ignition system that I thought would be an easy fix, but we would need to tow it home to Dale's house where I could fix it later in the week.

I had learned a lot about cars since an experience back in the summer of 1974 with my mom. That summer, Mom and I were planning our drive up north to Lakeport. The long way around, via Ukiah, was a hundred miles and fairly straight most of the way; whereas, it was only a seventy-mile trip if we decided to take the steep and curvy Hopland Grade Route. We were going to join my dad and brothers for a weekend of fishing on Clearlake. I hated the winding, mountainous Hopland Grade because it made me car sick and Mom was terrified of mountain roads, so we opted for the longer route.

Northbound we went, in our oil-burning 1958 Chevy Delray four-door sedan, one of the "fifty-dollar specials" we'd owned over the years.

The seventy-five degree day in Sebastopol became an eighty-five degree day by the time we reached Cloverdale, just forty miles north. Highway 101 coursed directly through the small town of Cloverdale and served as the town's Main Street.

We passed Dann's Owl Cafe, a stop for logging trucks that carried lumber south from Humboldt and Mendocino Counties to the Bay Area. As we drove slowly toward the end of town, I begged Mom to stop at Fosters Freeze, telling her that I really needed to pee. I knew that if we stopped at Fosters, I might get a soft-serve ice cream on such a hot day. Much to my delight, Mom pulled off to the left and into Foster's parking lot.

I went to the men's room while Mom suspiciously eyed the temperature gauge on the dash of the temperamental old Chevy. As I peed into the urinal, I read a poem someone had scribbled on the wall, "Don't change Dicks in the middle of a screw, Vote for Nixon in '72!" An interesting play on words, my adolescent mind thought, laughing aloud as I washed my hands and rejoined Mom outside.

I watched eagerly as the Softee machine squeeze out a swirling mixture of chocolate and vanilla ice cream into the cone. Mom opted for a plain vanilla, and we sat on a carved up, wooden bench outside, enjoying our treats.

"God, I hope it doesn't get any hotter today," Mom prayed aloud. We finished our ice cream cones and headed back to our car. I was all smiles, having been blessed with a rare treat.

As we continued our journey north, the temperature climbed as we drove along the Russian River, past the Black Cat Café. We tempered the heat with all four windows rolled down and the wing windows aligned for maximize airflow into the car. Old-timers called this "4-55 AC," when all four windows are rolled down at fifty-five miles per hour. Through Hopland, then Ukiah, we took the exit off Highway 101 onto Highway 20, where a billboard sign depicting a waterskier on a lake announced, "Lake Mendocino, Lake County Resorts."

As we climbed a long, steady incline to the Lake County line, the temperature gauge on the Chevy started climbing as well. If we could make it to the top of the hill, we would be home free since the downhill side, toward Blue Lakes and beyond, would provide some relief for the old Chevy's tired and overheated engine.

Mom was a nervous wreck anytime she drove a car under normal circumstances, white-knuckling the steering wheel with both hands and intently staring straight ahead at the road, only occasionally glancing down at the gauges or into the rearview mirror. She started talking to herself. I looked over, first at her panic-stricken face, then down to the rising temperature gauge.

"Don't worry, Mom, we're gonna make it. We're almost to the top of the hill and once we get headed back downhill on the other side, she'll cool down," I said, trying to her reassure. She ignored my remark as she intently alternated her cold stare between the rising red needle of the temperature gauge and the rearview mirror. She was talking to herself in mumbled, panic-stricken tones.

An unseen line of cars had built up behind us as Mom slowed down in an attempt to prevent overtaxing the engine. We were stuck in a bad situation. Nowhere to pull off the road to let the growing line of traffic pass but if she sped up, the car might overheat completely!

Apparently, all the prayers she learned through twelve years of Catholic schooling, back in Detroit, weren't working, because a slight, steady wisp of steam escaped from somewhere beneath the car's hood. The wisp became a flowing fog of steam and less than a quarter mile from the summit, it became evident that the ninety-five degree heat would win the battle with the old Chevy's corroded cooling system. Mom tearfully pulled off to the shoulder of the two-lane highway, fortunate there was a wide spot available, just as steam surrounded the entire hood and windshield of the car and the gauge pegged far to the right.

"Why does this always happen to me, why God?" she said clearly through tears of frustration and worry. At that moment, as if in response, the red "idiot light" illuminated itself as the hissing steam and powerful sounds of boiling water encompassed the old Chevy in a hot, steamy cloud of despair.

There I sat next to my crying mom, helpless to do anything to make things better, wanting to help, wanting to fix the car, and stop Mom's tears, but I couldn't do anything except sit next to her as she sobbed. As further insult and embarrassment, one of the cars in the line behind us that we had caused to slow down, went by slowly, and a man hung out the back passenger window and yelled angrily, "Keep that piece of shit off the road, asshole!"

Once the car cooled down over a period of about 30 minutes Mom fired it up and limped up the hill. The long downhill road ahead cooled the car down all the way to normal. In the trauma of the experience I made a promise to myself, right then and there, that I would learn how to fix cars. I swore I would do my best to make sure this helplessness and humiliation would never happen again.

Over the coming months and years, I kept that promise. I went to the Sebastopol Carnegie Library over a period of several months and studied copies of the Motor's Auto Repair Manual, a set of thick, blue hardcover books, available for every year vehicle made, from 1905 to 1972. In short order, I knew the tune-up specifications, horsepower and torque ratings, and cubic-inch displacements of every available motor for every make of car from 1955 to 1972.

I took auto shop and started out by taking apart and rebuilding a Briggs & Stratton lawn mower engine. I learned the fundamentals of the engine's four cycles or strokes, intake, compression, power, and exhaust, or as we called them in auto shop, suck, squeeze, bang, and blow. I was well on my way to becoming "Danny the Mechanic!"

So, in 1977, when it was time to trade my truck for the dune buggy, Brad hooked up a VW-style tow bar and attached the buggy to the hitch on my truck, which would soon be *his* truck. He used a small, round piece of wood to replace a missing metal pin. Having misguided faith in Brad's makeshift tow bar fix, off we went down Sonoma Mountain and followed Bennett Valley Road westward, toward Santa Rosa.

While thoughts of beach days flooded my imagination, a problem developed with the wooden replacement pin on the towbar. We were almost to the fairgrounds in Santa Rosa, on a straight stretch of Bennett Valley Road, when I caught movement out of my left peripheral vision. I was astounded when I turned to my left and saw the dune buggy roll parallel to the truck and into oncoming traffic! Oh shit, I thought, what do I do?

As if in slow motion, I watched the dune buggy, with what I hoped would be a gentle, slow stop against the steep left dirt bank of Bennett Valley Road, turn into a spectacular hill climb, flip upside down, and bounce back down on the pavement. The buggy flipped again and landed in the proper position on all four wheels!. What a miracle that there was no oncoming traffic and that nobody was hurt!

Dale and I looked at each other, stunned at what had just happened. The old truck we were in hadn't been fully converted from the original six-volt electrical system to a modern twelve-volt system, which meant the headlights didn't function. Dusk was approaching, so after making sure the slightly damaged dune buggy was completely off the road, we drove the truck the rest of the way home to get Dale's dad and his Chevy Blazer, to complete the tow of the buggy.

Once again, the tow bar was hooked to the dune buggy, but this time a metal bolt replaced the wooden pin when Dale's dad hooked it up to his Chevy.

When we were almost to Furlong Road and home, on a winding stretch of Occidental Road, disaster struck again. This time, the buggy came loose from the tow bar and hit a telephone pull. The impact essentially bent the dune buggy in half, destroying the fiberglass body beyond repair. We dragged the carcass of the dead buggy down Furlong Road with a chain and put it up in the horse barn at Newman's house. So much for bikinis on the beach!

The worst part was yet to come: to keep my word, I would have to give my truck and sole source of transportation to Brad, as promised. I pleaded with both Brad and his dad for their help. I had nothing—and no family who would or could help.

Brad and I had been inseparable from the age of ten up until two years prior, when his dad sold their apple ranch in Sebastopol and bought a vineyard on Sonoma Mountain. I was like one of the family and had worked for his dad bagging crushed ice at the ice trailer downtown at the Shell gas station in Sebastopol. I drove around with their dad in their VW van and their Pontiac Safari station wagon, to the ice house at Railroad Square in Santa Rosa and to his other ice trailers. The family often picked me up to go to various school and Boy Scout events. I thought, surely, I was not only Brad's best friend, but that his parents considered me part of the family.

Instead, my old best buddy and his dad said, "Tough luck, Danny, a deal is a deal, so bring the truck back." They screwed me, and it stung badly! I had no family, no money, and now I had no vehicle. Brad and his dad had the means to make sure I kept my truck; in fact, Brad had several other vehicles available to him. Instead, I learned a harsh lesson at 17 years old: I can't count on anyone.

Through that terrible experience, I learned I was on my own. My so-called "friends" weren't going to help me or do anything for me without a potential payoff for themselves. My fantasy of a triumphant return home to Sebastopol, where I would be warmly welcomed and nurtured, was shot down in flames. I realized in that moment that I was truly on my own.

Mr. Newman, Dale's dad, felt bad for me and helped by giving me a VW "pan," which is essentially the frame of a VW bug, so that I could attempt to fix the dune buggy. I eventually shortened the body with a cutting torch and welder by one foot to accommodate a new fiberglass body, if I could ever afford one. That's as far as I could go with it, since I had no money for a new fiberglass body.

I relied on Dale, who had his 1969 Buick GS from his sixteenth birthday, and his younger brother Jimmy, who inherited a 1966 Nova from his grandmother, for transportation until I could make some money and buy another car. I got a job washing dishes out at Negri's Italian Restaurant in Occidental, where Jimmy, Dale's younger brother and Dale were cooks. I rode to and from work, a few short miles away, with one or the other of them.

The Crew brothers, classmates and neighbors who lived near the Newman's, had a light mustard colored 1970 Mercury Monterey, sitting in a field near their house, surrounded by tall grass. The Merc was a former police vehicle, bought at auction after the agency painted over the black and white with yellow and removed the police equipment. They left the built-in spotlights, however—an amber light on the driver's side and a clear one on the passenger's side. The full sized car had a powerful 428 police special engine, which had skipped a tooth on the timing chain and left her field bound some months prior. I gave Mr. Crew $50.00 for the beast and somehow pulled it with a chain using Newman's Blazer to the auto shop at Analy High School. I hoped I could repair the old car and get her going again.

Once I tore into the 428 motor, it was a pretty easy job to replace the timing chain and gears. I put in a hot battery and sprayed in some starter fluid, expecting the old gal to reawaken. Unfortunately, the compression in the cylinders was too low to get her going. Mr. Conger, the auto shop teacher, suggested I take out each spark plug, one by one, and squirt a little transmission fluid in each hole to create a seal between the piston rings and the cylinder bore. Once she started pumping oil up into the top-end, she should be fine.

The idea worked like a charm and the old beast roared back to life as the boys in the shop and I whooped it up in celebration! A white cloud of smoke filled the area outside the school shop, as the transmission fluid burned in the engine. So Mr. Conger asked me to shut it down and come back after school, to warm it up completely and drive it home.

I came back to the shop after my last class when I could finally drive the Merc home. The car fired up instantly and the persistent white cloud of smoke reappeared out the tailpipes. The cloud became thicker and larger, like a plume of smoke, until I decided to get moving down High School Road toward Occidental Road and home. I put her into gear, and she tore out of the parking lot full of life, spewing out that white smoke like a dragon. The holes in the mufflers added an angry growl. I cruised along, filled with nervous excitement, when I heard a distant siren coming up from behind. Soon the flashing red lights appeared through the white haze, and I pulled off to the side of the road, thinking, Shit, what did I do?

As I exited the vehicle, the police officer greeted me with a smile on his face, radio in hand.

"Hello, sir, sorry about all the smoke, but my shop teacher had me squirt tranny fluid in the cylinders to start it. Looks like it's taking a while to burn it all out," I explained with a sheepish grin on my face.

The officer started laughing and said, "We had a report of a fire out here and I just happen to be out this way." He clicked his radio and told the dispatcher, "It's a kid's auto shop project out here. There's no fire!" He told me to have a safe drive home and wished me luck with the old Mercury. I glanced in the rearview mirror as I drove home and the white smoke persisted. It would blow at least a small amount of white smoke for a week of daily driving.

The old Merc was no "chick magnet," but it was at least a start in regaining my independence. I lusted after the 1968 Camaro SS 396 that Perry Alberdingi got for his sixteenth birthday and the 1969 Mach 1 that his buddy Sean Murphy had, and the 1969 Mach 1 390 with a four speed that neighbor Mark Wardlow bought after he sold his 1964 Impala SS. The $1200 cars of the time consisted of Camaros, Chevelles, Mustangs, Novas, GTOs, Firebirds, Dodge Chargers, and Plymouth Roadrunners.

I knew more about the cars than the kids who owned them, but that didn't mean a thing since I had no money to buy one for myself. I was in survival mode and the old CHP Merc would have to suffice for the time being. The hot girls seemed to like the guys with the hot cars, and I attached way too much of my self-esteem to a car; therefore, I was unworthy and a loser in my own mind.

I sat in class and knew I was one of the most capable kids in the room, but all the things I'd been told by my teachers at Twin Hills and by Boss Lady Jean back in the apple orchards—work and study hard to succeed—seemed to be bullshit. The dumbest kids had nice hotrod cars, the stupidest boys had the hottest girls, and here I was with nothing and no one.

Add to this situation the abrupt halt of my athletic aspirations, due to the near-death motorcycle accident that left me feeling like a spectator of life. My old football, baseball, and tennis buddies were playing, and all I could do was watch with envy. I was lost, yet I was also determined to ride out this low period in hopes of brighter days ahead. And that time would eventually arrive in my life, but not before things grew much darker in the days and months ahead.

In April of 1977, just two months after getting the hell out of Lakeport and away from my asshole dad, I received a morning phone call from my sister while I was getting ready to go to school.

As "Carry on my Wayward Son" by Kansas played in the background, I listened in shock as my sister's voice told me that Grandpa had died in his sleep during the night. I thanked her for the call as I hung up, my mind lingered over the lyrics still ringing out of the radio, *"Carry on my wayward son, there'll be peace when you are done, carry on my wayward son, don't you cry no more."* I cried like a baby. I didn't care that Jimmy and Dale were watching, as this was a deep pain I couldn't hide. "Damn, Gramps, why you and why now?" I said aloud to no one in particular.

In the pain and agony of repeated surgeries on my right arm during December 1976 after the November motorcycle accident, both of my great grandparents had died—first Grandma Jannie and ten days later, Grandpa Cleo.

Now, Gramps was gone too. Gramps had always been an island of sanity for me, and now I felt truly alone for the first time in my life. I would "carry on" for Gramps. I would become the man he and my father never were. How? I had no idea, I just knew that I would.

Waiting for the Sun

I FOLLOWED THE HIGH SCHOOL crowd and tried to blend in without drawing attention to myself. I began to feel like a burden and a reluctant addition to a family that had enough to worry about already. I ate sparingly and never asked for anything, lest I be told to leave. I narrowed my focus to just surviving and finishing high school.

A once loud and proud leader, I became a fly on the wall, with self-esteem lower than whale shit. I gravitated to the "stoner" crowd and smoked weed almost daily. I was stricken with the beauty of girls becoming women but much too shy to engage with any of them, other than an occasional wave while walking down the hallway between classes. School was easy for me, and I took all of the college prep classes, even though college seemed a distant dream. The teachers at Analy High School were supportive, and I even had an offer to occupy a cabin on the property of my old speech coach and assistant principal, Mr. Barrett. I chose the familiar, dysfunctional path by remaining at the turbulent Newman house.

Between my junior and senior years of high school, I worked with Dale's little brother, Jimmy and his dad, helping them set up a new auto body shop down in San Rafael and then, once the shop opened for business, washing the finished cars. I loved cars and thought I might become an apprentice body man or a painter, but I learned that "blood is thicker than water" when Jimmy's Dad, Jim Sr., wanted his son to learn the trade, not me. Jim Sr. did hook me up with a job as a helper for an electrician, and I learned a lot about electrical work. I continued working with the electrician for most of my senior year, going to school until 11:30 a.m. and then working in the afternoon.

The transmission in the old CHP car eventually gave out, so we pulled the motor and transmission out with a tractor, after cutting away the front end of the car with a torch. The neighbor kids used the body for target practice with rifles of every caliber, and when it was full of hundreds of bullet holes, we towed it out into the middle of Furlong Road and made an anonymous call to the sheriff about a loud gun battle down the road! The car was towed away after the sheriff units converged and found nobody around.

I got my fifty dollars' worth out of that car. We called her "the tank" because she was big and seemingly indestructible. Saturday night excitement, and a way for me to fit in and be part of the crazy crowd, started with a case of beer from Basso's Freestone Corner out in Freestone, along with a tank of gas. Six teens, beer cans in hand, cruised the back roads of western Sonoma County looking for mailboxes to "adjust."

The tank would take out a rural mailbox with style and flair. The wooden post would quickly break off, sending the instantly detached mailbox skyward. One bounce off the roof of the tank and that sent the lively teens laughing and whooping it up inside the car. "That was awesome, hit another one!" one of my excited and drunk passengers would say.

Out along the rural roads west of Sebastopol, I plowed down every mailbox in sight without regret or guilt. I was pissed off at the hand life had dealt me, and if I was going to lose the game, then at least I would destroy some shit along the way.

The guys with hot cars were bought for them by their moms and dads, the football games and excitement, and the girls taken out on dates and to school dances like the prom. All these high school trimmings were beyond and absent from my plate. Many of my lifelong friends from Twin Hills Elementary School were having the times of their lives as high school seniors; I most assuredly was not.

I placed so much of my self-image on the cars I drove and didn't drive. Seems silly now, but in high school back then, you *were* your car, at least as far as I was concerned. I knew more about the cars driven by their "turn-the-key-and-go" owners than the kids who were gifted them from their parents. I was a passenger who wanted to be the driver. I hated having to bum rides.

I felt like a scrounge, relegated to picking up leftovers and discarded scraps that other kids found useless. I felt like I was simply lucky to be alive and that I dare not ask for more. This was simply my fate, for now. I told myself, every day, to just survive this cloudy time and eventually the sun would shine again.

The chilly winter days awakened the pain in my right forearm as the cold stainless-steel plate attached to my bone throbbed, reminding me that I was weak and injured. I watched the football games at my high school with a combination of envy and sadness. Some of the players and old friends would get together after the games, but I no longer fit in with the jock crowd. I stayed in denial about the possibility of healing up fast and rejoining the team, but that was just a pipe dream.

At Thanksgiving, Mrs. Newman urged me to visit my family up in Lakeport. I was hoping to make enough money to last a few months of my final year of high school by selling a pound of pot that Dale fronted me to one of my old hot-rod buddies in Lakeport. When I arrived home, I was given a cold reception by my family. By this time, Mom had bought a house and Dad had lost his job at the radio station. Dad said I could sack out in my sleeping bag up in the garden shed at the corner of the yard.

I stashed the pound of smoke up on a shelf, behind some gallon cans of paint, while I cruised around town looking for my old buddy who I'd hoped was in the market for my weed. We smoked a joint and he agreed to buy the pound, so I went back to retrieve it from the garden shed. Much to my dismay, the pot was gone!

My brothers swore they had no idea where it had disappeared to, but I had my doubts. Years later I found out that, of course, Rich and John had ripped me off. If you can't trust your own brothers, then who can you trust? I bummed $10.00 from Mom for gas and left, disheartened and broke. Shit, how was I going to pay Dale for the weed now?

Back home at the Newmans home I started thinking about what the hell I was going to do after high school. I started hanging out with Brad Crew, one of the two brothers that had sold me the 1970 Mercury (a.k.a. the highway patrol/mailbox rammer) for fifty dollars. Brad and I took ground school for a private pilot's license through Santa Rosa Junior College. Brad was intent on joining the Air Force and I was tempted to join as well. When they told me I couldn't be a pilot without 20/20 uncorrected vision, I opted out.

Sister Deborah ended up at Palm Drive Hospital when her biker friend, Big Al, laid down his Harley out on River Road past Guerneville. Deb had the "road rash blues" from skidding across the pavement for several yards. Jimmy and I went to the hospital to see her, and we walked out the back with her and smoked a joint. She was crazy as hell, but I sure loved my sister and wished she would pick a new crowd to hang around. Maybe, I began to think, this was who we were, "born to lose" siblings, entertainment fodder for the "beautiful people?"

Finally, as the day of high school graduation was approaching, I went shopping at the Gap for Levi's at Coddingtown Mall, over in Santa Rosa. Having little to no money at this point, I did what I needed to do to get a new pair of graduation pants. I grabbed two pairs of the same pants from the rack and proceeded to the dressing room. After putting on the new pants and then my old pants overtop the new ones, I emerged from the dressing room with a single pair of pants, which I returned to the rack and then made a nervous exit.

"I brought you boys some Kentucky Fried chicken so you can eat something, because I know you'll be drinking tonight and you don't want to get sick!" said Mrs. Newman, as we readied for the big event on June 8, 1978, at 8:30 p.m. I was proud to be among the 289 graduates that night. After the ceremony on the football field, I watched as many classmates shared hugs with parents and relatives bearing flowers and gifts. I felt a mixture of sadness and relief as I headed over to Grange Hall for the graduation party. I drank and smoked and laughed with the crowd at Grange, all while the band played into the night.

I awoke at 4 a.m., out behind the building, when no one was around. I dusted off my drunkenness and started to walk home to the Newman home out on Furlong Road, about six miles away. There were no cars on the road at this time of morning or I would have hitched a ride, if possible.

I made my way slowly back through town and out by the 7-Eleven, a distance of two miles, when I spotted my old neighbor and cupcake crew buddy, Perry Alberdingi, in his 1968 Camaro. I flagged him down and hopped in, but he dropped me off only a half-mile later, at the end of Watertrough Road, saying he was late and in trouble already, so he couldn't drive me all the way out to Furlong. You son-of-a-bitch, I thought. I continued my walk in the cold night without a flashlight, two-and-a-half miles down and three-and-a-half miles to go.

Finally, I walked up the gravel driveway to the Newman house, just as the sun peeked out. I was looking forward to sleeping off a nasty hangover. There were Dale and Jimmy's cars and my 1966 Comet parked down in the field. I walked through the door and went to bed as Dale, no doubt hung over himself, snored away. Ah, finally I could lay down and rest.

After only a few minutes, there came a sharp knock on the bedroom door. "Time to wake up and time to get the hell outta here. You graduated now, so hit the road!" Dale's Dad exclaimed.

I didn't even involve myself in the argument that ensued between Dale and his dad. I just gathered up my few clothes and possessions, placed them into a cardboard box and walked down to my Comet, where I put them in the back seat and drove away.

The Long Road Home

MY MIND HAD BEEN SET on coming home for many years. I didn't know how or when, I only knew it was inevitable. It just so happened that my old childhood home down on the corner would soon be vacant. Once their tenet moved out, Dena, the Boss Lady's daughter and David, her husbands offered to let me look inside to spur old memories that might help my writing. I got to thinking later that day, Wow, wouldn't it be something if I could actually move back home after forty-three years to finish my book? Well, that's exactly what I did.

The rain had been relentless in 2019 and the first order of business was to replace the hot water heater in the basement, which had flooded and been ruined. Once the new hot water heater was installed, I scrubbed the grease, built up over years of cooking, off the walls, cabinets, microwave, and refrigerator in the kitchen.

I called in a plaster guy to fix the peeling plaster in the middle and front rooms. After the plaster was dry, I painted the ceilings, moved in some furniture, and slept in the back bedroom that my two little brothers and I had first shared forty-five years earlier. What a surreal feeling! I was home and loving it, as if in a dream or a memory, only now things were peaceful and quiet, no yelling, no arguing, no brothers wanting to fight—and no fear.

I looked at what was left of Gramps' cottage and I unexpectedly started to weep as the memories between those walls came back fresh and overwhelmed me. This little place had been my childhood refuge, an island of sanity when I needed to escape the house, and Gramps was always happy to see me and gently talk things over while I sat on his little gas heater.

Sometimes, I would sit next to him out here in the narrow workshop area and watch him write down morse code translations in his notebook and send out his own dah-dit-dah-dah-dit replies. He was never annoyed or bothered by my many questions. I snapped my attention back to the present day and realized that the very place where his chair sat had turned into dirt and rotten floorboards.

I grabbed a shovel and told an invisible Gramps that we'd get this place back into shape! I dug out years of dirt that gophers had pushed up through the floorboards and rotted them away, talking to Gramps, in my mind, the whole time. I found a dog medicine bottle from the 1900–1910 era, a Matchbox toy 1965 Dodge Tow truck, a few old wine bottles, and a couple of interesting rocks but mostly just wheelbarrow after wheelbarrow of dirt.

After the digging, I put new pier blocks, floor joists, and plywood down and leveled the cottage. New doors and windows, with a new high and open ceiling, made the cottage feel doubled in size. Fresh trim and paint, all new electrical outlets and fixtures, and a final thought was to add a small shower. Gramps would be proud and pleased that I'd helped keep his old place alive.

Out in the old garage, where my sister had kept her horses and the occasional chickens over the years, more digging awaited. David and Dena didn't believe it when I told them there was a cement floor under all that dirt. I knew because I'd shoveled out a foot of dirt, horse, and chickenshit decades before, so I could park my car inside.

There I was, at fifty-nine years old, doing exactly what I had done, in exactly the same place, when I was fifteen years old. I felt like I was fifteen again! And excited and grateful to have the opportunity to make something out of nothing again with a little elbow grease

Once the dirt was out and the cement was revealed, I could see that the one hundred-year-old cement floor needed help. I used self-leveling concrete epoxy to put down a smooth layer and fill in all the cracks over. I painted it and got the sliding door rolling again, so it would be ready for my 1967 "circled back home" Camaro! The Camaro was the car, right out of high school, that Jody, my first wife and mother of my four beautiful daughters, received from her dad. We went on our first date in that Camaro, chose a root-beer brown color and American Daisy Mag Wheel for it together, and subsequently brought our first two girls home from the hospital in it.

I wanted to take five-year-old Elizabeth and three-year-old Melissa to Disneyland for Elizabeth's Birthday in 1987, but funds were short for our young and growing family. The Camaro had just been sitting in the carport for a couple of years, so we sold it to a kid fresh out of high school for $1200. I'll never see that car again and thanks for the memories!

Fast forward to 2017 and I'm browsing old cars on Craigslist, when I come across a picture of a 1967 Camaro on a trailer, mostly with gray primer but with brown mixed in and sporting old, rusty Daisy wheels. No way, I thought, this couldn't possibly be the Camaro we sold in Lakeport thirty years ago and is now sitting in Fresno, or could it? I took a drive down to Fresno and right away I knew it was my old car—same 327 V8 with a 2-speed Powerglide, Rally Sport hideaway headlights, and the same interior. I had to have it back!

Yes, it needed lots of love, but what are the chances? Most old Camaros have been wrecked or converted into drag racers or flat track cars, but mine still lived. So now, all these years later and after a full restoration that I spent many hours of sweat performing, not to mention throwing out a few curse words along the way, the car in the old garage is my shiny, marina blue 1967 Camaro!

The daily walks over and down through the orchard, along the creek and back up the hill past the apple dryer and the big red barn and tall, white water tower, have been constant sources of memories and inspiration for writing.

The big red barn holds a special place in my heart, and I was saddened to see the state of disrepair it had fallen into. The roof on the south side looked like Swiss cheese, and everything inside on that half of the barn was wet, rusty, moldy, or rotten. David, who by this time I had affectionately started calling Big Poppy, and Dena, who so much reminded me of her mother, Jean, that I had just naturally started calling her Boss Lady, were both gracious and willing to save the barn and for that I am forever grateful! I took several wet and stinky loads of "God knows what" to a couple different hazardous waste sites. I loaded a dumpster full of crap, and I shoveled muck and cleaned out underneath the entire floor.

By this time, the Mexican workers stared at me like I was crazy; they had probably never saw an old white boy outwork a Mexican before, and they didn't quite know what to make of me. Big Poppy and the Boss Lady didn't know what to make of me either, despite my telling them how this was all a labor of love.

I was always so proud to live on the corner of Burnside and Watertrough when I was a kid, walking up to Twin Hills School and knowing all the kids who lived out in the countryside, riding the school buses and looking out the window as they passed my home, thinking, That's where Danny Dawson lives! The original owner of the Elphick Mansion, my Dad said, was one of the first, big-time apple growers in the area. I always thought people should see this beautiful house.

Once I added the picket fence to the top of the old solid fence and painted it white, my fence, as I envisioned, was complete. I was complimented on how it looked, because it opened up the front of the house. Now I could see people walking or bicycling by in front of the house and wave and say, "Howdy!"

The energy and happiness of my homecoming spread up past the barn as Big Poppy turned me loose on the Ford backhoe that had been sitting for at least twenty years. With a new battery and front tire, it fired right up. I spent days loading old concrete drainage pipes into dumpsters to clean up a berry bush-covered area under the apple trees, just to tidy up the place and be a good tenant.

Probably my biggest thrill since being home, other than Big Poppy giving me a tractor to use that saved my back, was the go-ahead to pull the 1925 Ford Model T Pickup out of the barn and turn a piece of would-be yard art into a smooth running, fun driving machine. I don't think Big Poppy had much confidence in my mechanical abilities, but his skepticism gave me all that much more motivation to get it poppin'.

New valves, new points on the sparky boxes, a good cleaning of the fuel system, and she fired up and ran! Everyone seemed impressed that I got the old truck running and I was feeling pretty proud. I jockeyed the hand lever into position while working the foot petals and adjusted the spark advance and throttle levers below the steering wheel, and off she went up toward the barn, where Big Poppy and Boss Lady were loading apple bins. All at once, and just yards from the barn, the right front, wooden spoke wheel showed its ninety-five-year-old age and folded up like a cheap Walmart tent. The front end took a dive into the gravel on her first drive, right there in front of an amused Boss Lady. Thereafter, Boss Lady referred to the old T as "Calamity Jane." Despite witnessing this event and once the tire issues were resolved, Dena was a good sport and went for a ride through the orchard in high gear.

After volunteering at the Community Apple Press down at Luther Burbank Farm and attending a couple of Western Sonoma County Historical Society meetings, I was talked into helping out with the Oral History Project by my third-grade teacher at Twin Hills School, Gloria Roberts. I met and took notes on Fred Bollinger and his 103-year life and history.

The last weekend in October brought a mass evacuation due to the Kincade Fire, way over across the Santa Rosa Plain and in the hills. "Evacuate my ass!" I said at 6 a.m. as strong winds blew smoke from the north and Highway Patrol bullhorns sounded up and down Watertrough and Burnside Roads. These idiots are stirring up a mass panic just to cover their political asses from the fire two years prior that burned Coffey Park.

My concern was for Big Poppy and Dena, if they were insistent on going, then the least I could do was to help them. I high-tailed it up the hill and went in the gate, waving to two Highway Patrol cars out in the middle of Burnside as the wind blew fiercely in the dark. I knocked on the door and when Dena saw that it was me, she broke down in tears of joy. The last person she wanted to see was a cop telling them to evacuate. We all felt confident that there was no way in hell that a fire in the hills above Cloverdale was ever going to reach us. That day and the "disaster" was the best day of the year. Power supplied by the diesel generator and the Boss Lady's excellent cooking skills made things nice and cozy and gave me a chance to get to know them better. I interviewed Big Poppy for the Oral History Project, and we talked about life, apple farming, and local history. As far as I was concerned, it was best damn natural disaster I'd ever encountered!

No home is home without a dog, and I got a beautiful and gentle golden retriever named Ruby in November. She's the funniest and sweetest exercise buddy I've ever had.

I cleaned up the old Darby house for David and Dena after a tenant moved out, and I had a blast discovering all the old paperwork and journals from the 1920s and 1930s, when Basil Darby and Henry Elphick ran the Apple Department of the Sonoma County Farm Bureau in the chicken coop.

In many ways, my homecoming was initially like returning to watch an old friend, almost unrecognizable now, slowly succumb to death. The old house on the corner had been hastily remodeled with Home Depot's finest and Gramps' cottage was barely left standing, with half of the old wooden floor rotted out and pushed up by years of dirt.

The south side of the big barn's roof looked like Swiss cheese and everything inside was ruined by years of water damage. The tall, white water tower was leaning precariously toward one corner and looked perilously close to falling. The roof of the labor shack at the sole remaining labor camp had folded in upon itself and water had done its work on the floor inside.

When I left the house in 1976, the rent was a hundred dollars per month, but now I was happy to pay $2000, in a county that had a medium-priced home of $825,000!

The Ghosts of Christmas Past

The short, cool days when the trees go bare mean Thanksgiving and Christmas is coming and, in our family growing up, you never knew what was going to happen. I remember a particularly significant Thanksgiving Day in 1972, when we extended the kitchen table all the way through the kitchen and into my brothers' and mine's bedroom to accommodate our extended family.

The celebration began the day before when we slaughtered a couple of the slower moving chickens and ducks. The ducks were hung by their feet and decapitated to collect the blood for a traditional Polish Czernina, a.k.a. Duck Blood Soup. This concoction had prunes and spices mixed with chicken broth, vinegar, and the duck blood base. I steered clear of it during the feast.

Great-Grandpa Cleo and Grandma Janie drove out from their little house in town. Gramps was here, too, along with aunts, uncles, and cousins from Dad's side of the family who all came to feast. This included Gramps' stepbrother Lowell, his stepsisters, Jackie Lee and Genevieve, and their husbands along with Jackie Lee's son, Randy. I loved my Grandma Janie, but she always wanted to kiss us kids on the lips, which wouldn't have been so terrible if not for the remnants of snuff on her lips. "Give me some sugar, Danny" she said as I looked at the wet snuff spots in the corner of her lips. Oh God, I'd just close my eyes and give her a quick peck. There were kids I didn't know from out of town, but we all became fast friends as we frolicked through the orchard, chased the chickens, and tossed around a baseball before the meal was ready in the house.

After the feast and all the cousins and others had gone home, Dad, Gramps, Great-Grandpa Cleo, and I stood in the living room in front of the fireplace where Dad announced, "Look at this, four generations of Dawson men here together today! Remember this, Danny, it's a pretty special day." If I would have known that the only generation still alive in eight years was going to be me, I would have savored the moment deeper and longer, but at twelve years old I had no idea.

Somehow, through the magic of Christmas, I am here again, in my childhood home, forty-seven years after that long ago feast. I'm looking at the beautiful Christmas lights, the decorations, and smelling the familiar, fresh scent of a tall, green Christmas tree placed in the front window, where four generations stood long ago in front of the fireplace and now seven stockings hang along the mantle for my grandchildren. The thing that quickly transforms me from a fifty-nine-year-old man into a twelve-year-old boy is the model train that encircles the Christmas tree. Lights and train whistle sounds accompany the clacking clack of the wheels as they pass quickly over the tracks that I meticulously laid out. The train winds through a scene that includes carefully placed porcelain buildings—a church with a tall steeple, a general store, and a couple of two-story Victorian houses, a horse and buggy—and figures of people walking with packages and children playing in the snow on a wooden sled.

Outside the sky is gray and overcast, and the recent rain has made the air clean and clear. The once powdery orchard soil has darkened, and the trees are full of fluttering golden leaves. There are apples, mostly rotted from last summer's crop, that feed the hungry birds that didn't fly south for the winter.

I feel very fortunate this Christmas! How many people can relive a Christmas in their childhood home, owned by a family not your own, a half a century later? A home never owned by my family. I would guess, very few, if any. I think this circumstance speaks to the power of the heart, the will to be healed, and to persistence and serendipity.

This time around, this Christmas finds the house filled with love and appreciation, kindness, hope, gratitude, and encouragement. Where there was drama, tension, and harsh words, there is today a pervasive calmness, a laughter devoid of tension and there are softly spoken words. There is no room here for alcoholic rants or unkind words. The only physical contacts are made in love, reverence, and appreciation. This house is quite different today, this is my home.

My first Christmas back here brought back a flood of childhood memories. I don't have to make up a phantom list of Christmas gifts received this time around, a list my 12-year-old self would rattle off over the phone to my friend Mark Swanson, who came from the kind of family I could only dream of having.

"Oh, you know Mark, the usual stuff, clothes, some new Hot Wheels and track, a couple of new books, a chemistry set, and a few board games." Then he would reply, in a bored tone of voice, "I got a new pair of Converse® All Stars and a basketball warm-up suit . . . "

My brothers and I solved the Christmas money problem using good old- fashioned American free enterprise! Mom bought us a few rolls of cheap Christmas wrapping paper from Longs Drugs and a couple of boxes of clear, plastic sandwich baggies, into which we put a square of the fancy Christmas paper and a sprig or two of mistletoe, gleaned from the low apple branches out in the orchard. We made up about fifty or sixty bags and headed down to Fiesta Market. "Would you like some Christmas Mistletoe for only twenty-five cents?" Richie politely asked a woman who exited the store with a cart full of groceries. "Oh, thank you, young man, I will have two!" she replied as she fished two quarters out of her coin purse. We sold out in a couple of hours and walked back home after splitting up the day's take that amounted to five dollars each and bought a candy bar and soda from inside the store. Plenty enough to buy Christmas presents downtown on Main Street!

Christmas shopping for Richie, John, and I began at Analy Rexall Drugs, next to the Shell gas station downtown, directly across Main Street and the railroad tracks from Carlson's Department Store. The pharmacy had lots of little gift items and a great record album selection too. I bought a small box of chocolates and a "Soap on a Rope" for Gramps and a little spray bottle of perfume for sister Debbie before leaving the pharmacy for Sprouse-Reitz, the "five and dime" store next door. It had a variety of seemingly unlimited trinkets and gifts. Personal items like nail clippers, combs, brushes, and reading glasses filled small display bins along the walls. The aisles were well stocked with playing cards, jacks, marbles, dice, board games, toys, boxes of candies, snow globes, wrapping paper, ribbons, and bows. The kitchen aisle had everything you could think of for cooking, canning, and eating. I bought a six-pack of little yellow plastic corn cobs with two sharp points on the end, which were used to insert into the ends of your corn on the cob so you wouldn't burn your fingers or get butter on them. I also bought a set of spoons in various sizes and some dish towels with "Merry Christmas" brightly embroidered on them. In the craft supplies aisle I picked out two balsa wood glider airplane kits, one for each of my two brothers and a plastic model of a horse for Debbie.

Walking south on Main Street, I went into People's Music and stared at the guitars hung up along the wall and smiled at the drum set on the floor before making my way to the awesome selection of record albums, all alphabetically organized in the display. I leafed through the B's to look at the Beatles album covers—*Yellow Submarine, Rubber Soul, Sergeant Peppers*, and *Meet the Beatles*. Randomly, I went through the albums looking at the artwork and pictures on their covers, imagining what sounds might be contained on the thin, black vinyl records that they held inside. Once I had finished gawking at the musical instruments again on my way out of the store, I walked back across Main Street. I just had to make a quick stop at Pease Pharmacy on the corner. I stepped up onto the large man-sized scale to see where the needle would land today. "Eighty-two pounds and still growing!" I said to nobody. I loved the old brass scale and the warm dark wooden walls at Pease and especially the phone booth inside the store, where I would occasionally call a friend just because I thought it was cool. Across Bodega Highway and on the corner was at my favorite store on Main Street: Western Auto.

I don't know why they called it Western Auto, because all I remember about the store was walking across the old, creaky wooden floor to look at the Western Flyer bicycles, all lined up on the floor, and then walking through the sporting goods section to the wall where rifles were displayed. The shelves were stocked with toys, games, and gadgets of every kind, just like in their Christmas catalog that we had at home. I had my eye on the Crossman Pump action .177 Pellet Gun up on the wall, perfect for hunting the annoying gophers back home in the orchard. I dreamed and sighed. No way would that beauty find its way under our Christmas tree . . . or would it? Gramps, sympathetic to my cause, encouraged me not to give up hope.

Christmas arrived and the early morning began with sneaking out for a peek at the tree in the living room. I scanned the back walls and under the tree, looking for a long box that would contain the pellet rifle from Western Auto, but nothing stood out. It wasn't long before Mom and Dad woke up and came out into the living room while my brothers and I ran quickly back to our room. "Come on out. We heard you boys out here already," Dad said. We scrambled out and under the tree in a frantic search for gift packages bearing our names as Mom started a pot of coffee and Dad took a seat on the living room couch after saying to me, "Danny, go out and get your Grandpa." Wrapping paper flew and laughter filled the room as I returned with a still half-asleep Gramps in his robe and slippers. Mom came in with coffee for Dad and Gramps while I watched my brothers and sister by the tree smiling and having fun. Mom told me to get the gifts marked "Dad" and "Grandpa" and bring them over to the couch for them. After all the fanfare and excitement had died down, Dad said, "This was your Grandpa's idea, go over and look in the back corner behind the tree." All eyes were on me as I spied the tall box in the corner. Could it really be a BB gun, I wondered. Yes—and not just any BB gun, but the coveted Crossman .177 pellet/BB combo pump action rifle from Western Auto that I had dreamed about for months. Gramps came through for me. He did it! That was the best childhood Christmas of my life! I did not have to make up a phantom list of gifts for my friends that year or envy anything my friends had received, not that year. I had received something I wanted for once and I was a very happy kid.

Despite all the renovation and love that I'd poured into my childhood home, I woke up from my Hilraeth fantasy and realized there was nothing here for me anymore. Try as I may, I was unable to make this little old house my own, even after offering a million dollars, my left testicle in a Mason Jar, and a commitment to watch out for the Boss Lady's daughter for the rest of her days. Dreams die hard and this one died painfully.

I woke up and took a good look around, rooted fully in the present moment. The unfenced rolling hills of apple orchards have been uprooted, burned, and turned into fenced-off vineyards as far as the eye can see. Politicians, drunk on the success of a tourist-based economy, turn a blind eye to the supplanting of dry farmed apples to water thirsty wine-grapes. Now, droves of tourists on bicycles compete for space on narrow backroads in the quest to engage in the new sport of "wine tasting" at the eight hundred wineries, scattered throughout the region.

Now, machines and Mexican laborers harvest grapes while an entitled younger generation play video games or attend camps in Occidental while on break from charter schools (Sonoma County has the most in any California county). McMansions dot the hillsides, and downtown is crowded with rich hippies who were once poor anti-establishment, free-land movement hippies. That is until they inherited property from their "square" parents, made a bundle, and now seek to protect their "rights" and property against any and all perceived intruders. Homelessness abounds with haphazard tent/cardboard cities, pushed from one place to another in "Whac-A-Mole" style by a clueless and inept government. The old free-love hippies are now no-love NIMBYs (Not In My Back Yard). They think having a "Namaste" bumper sticker and a white ponytail makes them progressive and superior.

My dream of coming home and farming a few acres of apples has become impossible in a new and monied wine country. The hometown that I grew up in is gone, the three-dollar cheeseburger downtown at Fosters Freeze is now a twenty-five dollar burger with gruyère cheese and an organic beef patty or a vegan deluxe. The train down Main Street that once carried carload after carload of apples destined for the San Francisco Bay Area is now gone, its train tracks erased by pavement. Bumper to bumper traffic on Hwy 101 is all too "normal" now, and the days of camping along the Russian River on a free pull-off spot are nonexistent. Service workers are crammed ten to twelve in a house just to afford the sky-high rents. Frustration, depression, and violence are the natural responses to the lack of opportunities. By the shrinking middle class and the younger generation. Family dynamics have changed tremendously as parents ask themselves, Would these kids keep such cozy relations with us if we didn't have property to leave them when we die? Those of us who have no property ask ourselves, Would my kids be around more if I had property to pass to them? Have I failed in life? Have I failed my family? Will the kids of the property owners take the money and burn themselves out to an early death through substance abuse and dangerous living?

I have raised four beautiful, intelligent, and compassionate women who are my daughters. These women and the five girls and four boys that they are now raising are my legacy. All of them are "priced out" of this place I call home, despite being elements of the very fabric of a civilized and functioning society. They are a certified public accountant, a mental health doctor, two registered nurses and their partners, two policemen, and a carpenter. What kind of community has this become? A private club for old, white hippy transplants from San Francisco? A walk down to Ives Park to hear live music for a "Peacetown Concert" confirms this truth. The few young people left in town walk around, sedated by wine, high-potency cannabis, and hard cider in a kind of survivors' guilt trance.

I fear for what will become of the apple town I once knew without a diverse population, diverse agriculture, and diverse opportunities. I fear the continued separation of people based on the wide gap between the have nots and service workers versus the "I got mine so screw you" monied elites.

The story of our hometown is much like inviting a bunch of rich city friends to your country home, only they decide to stay and never leave. They invite some of their friends until your own home is unrecognizable. They replace your old, comfortable furniture with new fancy stuff and replace your appliances with good intentions, but it all just feels wrong somehow.

At some point that old house becomes trashed and abandoned. There is no water to drink because all the residential wells have gone dry, the vineyards simply had a longer and thicker straw into the same water source as the common people. The landscape is barren now, having been thoroughly raped and abused since the roaring days of wine and roses.

The money, the parties, and the good times have moved on to ravage the next frontier of exploitation. It was fun while it lasted! My gravestone, to be placed up by Charles Schulz of "Peanuts" fame, a mile up the road, will read, "Here lies Danny D. He finally found an affordable piece of Sebastopol country real estate."

Pictures of Home

139

About the Author

DANIEL GREW UP IN THE small Apple Farming Community of Sebastopol, CA and completed his education at Sonoma State University. He worked at the world's largest Geothermal field during the boom years until it started to lose steam. Consulting and municipal assignments have enriched his life with varied and interesting experiences. He is the proud father of four beautiful and accomplished daughters and nine grandchildren and a proud renter in his childhood home in Sebastopol, part of the new Wine Country, where he works pro bono for various farmers and businesses keeping the Apple alive.

CPSIA information can be obtained
at www.ICGtesting.com
Printed in the USA
LVHW021023170322
713598LV00007B/606